Harry Turner has been a salesman all his working life. After service as a young army officer in Austria, he became a canned food salesman in London's East End – an experience neither to be missed nor repeated. This was followed by a five-year stint in Fleet Street selling advertising space for the *Daily Herald*, *Sunday Graphic* and *Sunday Times*. In 1960 he joined *TV International Magazine* as Advertisement Manager but managed to write a few feature articles at the same time. In 1962 he joined Westward Television Sales Department where he spent nineteen years, becoming Sales Director in 1972. Since 1981 he has been Director of Sales and Marketing for Television South West.

His two other great passions are writing and world travel. He has over two dozen short stories in print; his story 'Hell's Bells' was made into a half-hour TV drama by Universal TV in Hollywood and 'The Tunisian Talking Ferret' was adapted for radio in Johannesburg. He writes a regular monthly gossip column for *Media World* and contributes life-style articles to *Campaign* and *Marketing Week*. A regular traveller to America, he has also visited Japan, Russia, Turkey, Thailand, Barbados, North Africa, Yugoslavia, Canada and Greece. His ambitions are to keep selling, writing, riding and playing tennis until he's ninety-four and never to visit Barnsley.

Harry Turner is married with a son and a daughter – one a fisherman, the other an artist. He lives in Surrey most of the time and in his house in southern Spain the rest of the time.

D0274134

Harry Turner

The Gentle Art of Salesmanship

Fontana Paperbacks

First published by Fontana Paperbacks 1985

Copyright © Harry Turner 1985

Set in Linotron Times
Made and printed in Great Britain by
William Collins Sons & Co. Ltd, Glasgow

Contents

Introduction

For those of us who have chosen it as a career, selling is about the most fun you can have with your clothes on. On the other hand, for the great majority who don't sell for a living it is an occupation with slightly less appeal than having your sinuses drained.

This book is dedicated to the former, to the existing salesman or saleswoman who still believes the really big order is just around the corner. Also, to the beginner; the hopeful with stars in his eyes who knows in his water that even flogging latex underwear in Macclesfield is infinitely more exciting than becoming an accountant.

Although the world has changed, the role of selling remains paramount. Clever engineers and clever scientists keep on inventing things – minicomputers, underwater power stations, musical contraceptives, chest wigs, candlewick loo covers. Not one of these things 'sells itself', a phrase much used by non-salespeople. Somebody has to go out and make the pitch. That moment, that magical snapshot in time when the sales proposition is offered and accepted, is the true fulcrum of mankind's endeavour. Compared to that, Sir Isaac Newton, Leonardi da Vinci, Alexander Graham Bell are just small potatoes. And don't you forget it. A selling career, as I shall · demonstrate in ensuing chapters, is good for your health, can make you rich, possibly famous, and offers unrivalled opportunities for world travel, good food, fine wine and sexual encounters undreamed of by quantity surveyors even in Slough.

1. The Qualities You Must Possess or Develop to Become a Megasuccess

Smile, nobody buys anything from a misery guts

Are salesmen born? Or can they be made?

There is no neat, black and white answer to this question. Certainly, without *determination* and the *will to win*, no amount of training will turn you into a demon salesman. You've got to *want* success so much you can almost *smell* it. Determination, therefore, is the engine that drives you towards achieving your goals. On the journey you will acquire knowledge, technique, social skills, cunning and ruthlessness. Don't shudder. You need all of those things in abundance if you're going to reach for the stars.

I am always most impressed with young salespeople who display determination, coupled with a tangible hunger for knowledge. Nobody ever learns it all, not even those sales wizards who get to the top of the heap. So, mistrust anybody who tells you they know all the answers: they're either a knave or a fool.

Thus, fuelled by determination and thirsting for knowledge, you now have to recognize those things that motivate people to become high performers. Number one is greed. Yes, *greed*. What's that? You heard it was a desire to perform a useful service to society? Who's been stuffing your head with that nonsense? Greed is OK. It's a potent force in pretty well all walks of life. Politicians are greedy for power, but they try to disguise it. They trick it out in fancy clothes and try to smuggle it past you, hoping you won't notice.

You too will have to temper your own greed, your own avaricious longing for success, and make it blend into acceptable forms. That's socially inevitable. But don't kid yourself it's not there. It is. Remind yourself each day, 'I'm greedy for success.'

Ambition is the other side of the same coin. You should genuinely aim for the stars, and think big. And don't be ashamed of wanting *material* rewards – a better car, a grander home, luxurious holidays, fine food, vintage wines. There's nothing wrong with any of those things. We live in the *real* world and, remember, your life is not a rehearsal. This is the only shot you're going to get at it. So identify just what it is you want and run like hell to obtain it. Try an occasional *taste* of luxury just to keep your appetite keen – and it's never too soon to appreciate the fine things of life.

When I was twenty and serving as a British officer in Vienna, I walked along a fashionable street one winter's evening looking at the grand eighteenth-century houses which had opened up again after the war years. Behind the brightly lit windows I could see elegant people sipping drinks, I could observe the curl of their cigar smoke, note the glitter of the women's jewellery. I was transfixed, it was like snatching a secret glimpse of some magical fairyland. My companion, another young officer, gave me a nudge. 'Settle down,' I remember he said, and we moved on to a noisy tavern for a couple of beers.

His phrase 'settle down' implied that such scenes of opulence which we had just witnessed were not really for us, and that any notions I might have of one day achieving a similar life style were fatuous in the extreme.

But I have never settled down. Neither should *any* salesman. He should *want* to be on the *inside* looking out – not *outside* like us on that Viennese pavement, gazing inwards with hopeless longing. Now I don't pretend for a moment that I own a fine mansion in Vienna, or anywhere else for that matter, but I refuse to accept that such aspirations are unreasonable. The true salesman *knows* that the best is still to come. His glittering mansion *is* just around the corner. Keep wanting it. Badly. It sharpens your sales performance, believe me.

Can being a 'snob' actually help you in your sales career? At first glance such a proposition may seem ludicrous. Snobbery is a bad thing, isn't it? Or is it? Let's start by defining just what the word *really* means. It means not accepting second best in your own terms. It means refusing to suffer fools at all, let alone gladly. It means the pursuit of excellence.

What's that? Snobbery means a whole lot of other, rather nasty things to you? That's *your* problem, sunshine, not mine.

Why should you *pretend* to like eating crap in a cheap restaurant when you can enjoy a gourmet meal in Paris? Must you cravenly admire the gross bad taste of some no-hoper living in Willesden when he shows you his illuminated plastic cocktail cabinet? And do you *really* prefer driving a beat-up Volkswagen to a Mercedes 500 SE?

Let's pause here, because you're probably shying away from the idea of being a salesman after all. I mean to say, greed, ambition, snobbery? Sounds awful, doesn't it? I've hammered these points home – perhaps crudely – because it is essential that you recognize them as *necessary* ingredients in your make-up if you're truly going to succeed. But certainly they will need to be tempered with many other qualities to complete the ensemble.

You see, it's perfectly possible for you to possess these dark hungry appetites as long as they are harnessed to things like style, wit, intelligence, knowledge and a sense of balance.

The myriad ingredients which make up the whole man are interdependent and feed from each other. Greed breeds ambition. Ambition breeds knowledge. Knowledge breeds confidence, confidence breeds style, style breeds acceptability, and so on.

Perhaps the single most *important* attribute a salesman must develop is a *love of language*. Not everybody has a natural gift for vocabulary, but the dedicated salesman must treat words like *gold-tipped ammunition*. Words paint pictures, remember, and these glorious images enable even the most prosaic proposition to become acceptable to the sceptical client.

You've heard the unflattering description, 'He's got the gift of the gab.' If somebody says it about you, rejoice. It is a 'gift', and if you've got it, hang on to it, polish it, hone it, develop it, cherish it.

So here you are on the threshold of greatness. Greedy, ambitious, snobbish, articulate, witty, knowledgeable, confident, determined. OK, what should you look like?

Must you be tall? Handsome? Beautiful? Not really. The *inner dynamism* that springs from those individually rather dodgy qualities I have listed will overcome all but the most ghastly physical handicaps. I've met some excruciatingly dumb, boring models, both male and female, who looked simply fantastic, but beneath the glossy surface – zilch.

Of course, if you're one of Nature's slobs, with bad teeth, halitosis, pimples and a hump, maybe you should forget selling and take up crematorium design or baggage handling at Gatwick Airport.

The best salespeople exude confidence and are good company. This doesn't mean they fire off a machine-gun repertoire of dirty jokes (that's the hallmark of a deadbeat salesman), but they are fun to be with. They smile a lot. Genuinely. Nobody ever buys anything from a misery guts.

The famous Dale Carnegie, who wrote the bestselling *How to Win Friends and Influence People*, counselled salespeople to practise smiling at their reflection in the bathroom mirror each morning before they went to work. I know it sounds a bit old-fashioned now – crass even – but a smile, if it's *real*, can still work wonders. The great commercial salesmen of the twentieth century, like Carnegie, are really actor-managers. They know they have to dominate the stage, call the shots and capture the imagination of their audience.

OK – is this cheerful, smiling persona compatible with greed, ambition, etc.? Yes it is. They are brothers and sisters under the skin.

What other questions must you ask yourself before embarking on a sales career? Perhaps it would be helpful if I gave you my identikit for the ideal salesman or saleswoman.

He or she must want success so much it *hurts*. They must be like sponges in absorbing knowledge about their chosen field *and* the world around them. They must not be ashamed of luxury and conspicuous consumption. They *must* be good talkers, witty, urbane – *interesting*. They will read a lot: novels, magazines, newspapers. They will have a sense of the 'theatrical'; of acting and putting on a performance. They will ooze confidence from every pore. They will be impatient, restless and unsettled. They will rarely live within their means. (Debt – in reasonable amounts – is a remarkably effective spur to greater sales effort.) They will be conscious of their physical appearance *and* its limitations, and have a finely developed dress sense. They will have 'high profile' personalities that make them easily distinguishable in a room full of sanitary engineers or bank cashiers.

They will be sensitive to other people's moods and fears, yet possess the hide of a rhinoceros. (If the prospect of being occasionally told to drop dead curdles your blood, become a lighthouse keeper.)

They will find sex a *major* factor in their lives.

What's that again?

They will find sex a major factor in their lives. Oh, really? No, this doesn't mean lunging at every customer of the opposite sex, but sexual desire is a life force and the personality of a *successful* salesperson often acts as an aphrodisiac.

It has been widely accepted that *power* and *success* are great sexual magnets. If you enjoy your life and your work is your life – if you are stimulating and aware and enthusiastic – the chances are you'll feel randy a lot of the time too. Salesmen get laid more than accountants . . . you'd better believe it!

Of course, the veritable cornucopia of qualities I have so far described as being essential to any future superstar salesman do manifest themselves in very different ways.

In some, the ingredients fuse together like a well-shaken cocktail and emerge in the form of a fizzing, extrovert personality. These salesmen are usually impressive talkers, they have an easy charm and often a strong physical presence. They know how to win by intimidation. They bludgeon their way to the top with a fair degree of ruthlessness. They are the *tigers*. More about them in a moment.

Others digest the complexities and contradictions of character that lie deep inside every salesman and they eschew the noisome, flashy style of the tigers, preferring a more cunning, cerebral approach. These salesmen can be insidiously persuasive. They understand the intricate chess game that goes on between buyer and seller and they can wield logic like a surgeon's scalpel. They can be physically unimpressive, even vulnerable-looking. They succeed by thinking two moves ahead of the competition. They are the *foxes*.

Most salespeople fall into these two very broad categories. Of course, there will be various shadings and overlappings, but it is easy to see whether you are a tiger or a fox by glancing at this checklist of characteristics:

Tigers

Physically strong
Highly articulate, extrovert
Fashion conscious
Weak on detail
Weak on planning
A tendency to be gregarious
Sociable, a shade flashy
Theatrical, good platform speaker
A fondness for food and drink
A keenness for sport or exercise (to counterbalance the above)

Foxes

Softly spoken
Physically unimpressive, but neatly dressed
Thoughtful, even scheming
Brilliant at detail
Strong on planning
Retentive memory for minutiae
Most effective in one-to-one sales situations
Quietly fanatical about succeeding
Bookish, music-loving

Foxes excel in jobs that require a high degree of technical knowledge. They are the ace computer salesmen, the high-fliers in aerospace systems, medical supplies, machine tools, radar equipment, information technology. In these complex fields *detailed product knowledge* is critical. The actual selling process is seldom spectacular. It's all relentless application, quiet authority, number-crunching, low-profile stuff. But beneath the surface is a glint of steel. The fox *knows* his store of intellectual weaponry will see him through. He uses logic, never emotion. He *demonstrates* and provides back-up evidence in mind-numbing profusion. He never gives up. He does all his homework himself. His friends are civil servants, solicitors, electronics engineers. He is a pain in the arse.

The tiger understands how to generate excitement. He paints a broad canvas, using imagery and magic. He is usually found selling concepts and big ideas. His adrenaline surge makes him a dazzling platform performer. He sells advertising (either space or agency creative work), expensive real estate, fashion goods, yachts, executive jets, holidays, racehorses. He has other people back at the office who do his number-crunching. His friends are actors, journalists, striptease artists. He prefers to screw *before* dinner, but *after* a half-bottle of Dom Perignon. He needs to watch his weight, his liver and his overdraft.

Today, the foxes outnumber the tigers. It's the way the world is going. If you can combine the primary characteristics of both fox and tiger you will be unstoppable.

So much for the foxes and the tigers. What about the vixens and the tigresses? We will examine them in the chapter 'Women in Sales'.

Meantime, here's another checklist. This time it shows the common characteristics that both foxes and tigers *must possess*.

Determination
Authority
Sincerity
Industry
Toughness
Hunger

Both fox and tiger must also acquire a touch of the chameleon. Each sales situation is slightly different from the previous one; each customer is an individual. Moods change. Economic climates rise and fall. All salesmen have to gauge the environment in which they are selling *at the precise moment they are making the pitch*. Even the most extrovert tiger will have to temper his exuberance if his prospect is a half-dead transsexual with piles who has just received a final demand from the Inland Revenue. Some prospects relax over a good lunch. Others don't eat lunch at all. Find out from the prospect's secretary *before* you book a table for two at Maison Pancreas – you could be wasting your company's money.

Sometimes a fox has to pretend to be a tiger. But only briefly. If the client is a noisy trencherman who pinches his secretary's bottom and supports Tottenham Hotspur, he may not appreciate the cerebral approach.

The trick is how to adjust without falling completely out of character. Even a fox can laugh and tell a joke. Even a tiger has to listen occasionally and allow his client to hog the limelight. But one *must* be careful.

I once knew a fox who switched from selling electronics to selling yacht charters. For years he had developed the low-profile style necessary to impress engineers who regard Hush Puppies and string vests as the height of fashion. He was a wizard at detail. He could drone through sheets of technical specifications over a ham sandwich and a plastic beaker of machine coffee without flinching. He answered all questions *precisely*. He learned to regard Crawley New Town in Sussex and Bracknell in Berkshire as 'beautiful places to work'. He made love to his wife once a week under the covers with the light off – and he found conjuring up visions of printed circuits was an invaluable aid to orgasm.

Then he became a tiger. Or tried to. He grew his hair long, bought a silk suit from Cecil Gee, invested in a gold Rolex watch, flogged his Rover 2000 and hocked himself up to the eyebrows in order to obtain a fifth-hand Jaguar.

The result was traumatic. The target market for expensive yacht charters is a million light years away from what he had been accustomed to. The new clients didn't give a stuff for the technical dimensions of a yacht or its depth of keel. They wanted *excitement*, *glamour*, *adventure*. A bit of flash. They craved the ego-polishing thrill of sipping dry martinis on the afterdeck surrounded by girls with thighs as strong as nutcrackers. They wanted to be told how the sleek, gleaming hull would slice through the azure blue waters of the Mediterranean from Monte Carlo to St Tropez whilst white-jacketed stewards served caviare under a blazing sun.

What they got instead was this no-hoper with dandruff, in a shiny suit, smoking a frayed cigar and forcing them to thumb through sheets of statistics about weight-to-speed ratios and wind resistance.

He made no sales. People began to avoid him. His reaction was pure knee-jerk. He produced even more technical data, blueprints of the yacht at design stage, engineer's reports, analyses of the radar systems that had been fitted to the bridge. After eight months without sales he was fired. His replacement was a younger man with *no technical knowledge whatsoever*. But he could discuss vintage wines and he knew the names of the head waiters at L'Oasis in La Napoule and the Grill Room at the Hôtel de Paris, Monte Carlo. He also knew how to write down yacht charters as a tax-deductible expense. And how to meet young women in bikinis no bigger than a child's handkerchief.

The same kind of disaster can befall a tiger who tries to become a fox. He can *briefly* and *temporarily* take on some of the characteristics of a fox. He can even pretend to be one, as I have already said – but he can *never* successfully *become* one. Why he should want to in the first place is a bit of a mystery, but it does happen. And it's horrible.

Strong men stagger and faint when I tell the story. It's true in every particular. A cautionary tale even more awful than that of the wretched electronics rep turned yacht salesman.

A tiger of my acquaintance married a lovely girl whose father owned a small company which made printing machinery. Previously, my friend had been a top salesman for an international fashion house. Father-in-law's loot seduced him into switching jobs and he became a machinery rep.

I met him for a drink in the Ritz two months after he had made the change. The elegant suit and the Gucci loafers had disappeared. So had the monogrammed shirt from Turnbull and Asser. Instead of the slim, soft leather briefcase with the brass fittings, he carried a fat Gladstone made of PVC. His tan – which was normally of Mediterranean hue – had vanished. A biro protruded from his breast pocket and, the final bone-chilling humiliation, he was wearing a nylon drip-dry shirt.

I forced a few drops of champagne between his lips and gave him the best advice he ever had. Quit. He did. Fortunately, his wife stood by him and he quickly rejoined his old firm where he is now Director of Marketing in Paris, living in an elegant apartment near St Germain and driving a blood-red Ferrari. But it was a narrow escape.

Moral. If you *know* you're a tiger – or a fox – don't try and become something that goes against your own personal grain.

Clients can sniff out a phoney very quickly. Even dumb clients. So, be yourself. Embellish, by all means. Trim, polish, duck, weave, react to special circumstances by a touch of fine tuning, *but stay true to your basic character*. If you don't, you'll end up like my friend nearly did.

2. What to Sell?

OK, so you want to sell for a living. First of all you've got to find something really interesting to flog. Some people can wax hysterically enthusiastic over porcelain hip baths and will scorch over their territory like dervishes with increasingly fat order books. Others revel in the sale of abstract ideas or monumental concepts. Somebody, remember, *persuaded* Egypt to build the Aswan Dam. No, it *didn't* just happen. A salesman or group of salesmen set the Egyptian authorities alight with enthusiasm for the idea. The hardware, the technology and the megatons of cement came later.

So, think about what fires you up in life and force yourself to analyse what stuns your brain with boredom. Reject the latter and pick a field that gives you the magical lift. Here's a helpful checklist to assist your decision.

Abstract	Tangible
Space sales for newspapers, magazines; airtime sales for TV, radio	Baked beans
	Cement
	Industrial oils
Life insurance	Real estate
Unit trusts	Rivets
Investment packages	Pet food
Expensive cars	
Holidays	

Not a definitive list by any means, but it does demonstrate the division between two very distinct types of selling.

If you are a *single discipline* salesman, your tidy mind will prefer a *limited* range of product, in a clearly defined market – like a life insurance rep. Although he is selling an *abstract*, i.e., protection, *future* benefits, etc., his battery of financial products are all closely related.

Although insurance reps will hate me for saying it, fear plays a large part in motivating people to buy insurance. What happens to the kids if I die? Supposing I get laid off from work, fall sick?, and so on.

The skilful life insurance salesman therefore needs to know a lot about human psychology. He needs to be a good listener as well as a good talker. He needs the ability to appreciate the hidden fears and unspoken worries of the ordinary family man. He needs to be willing to sit in an uncomfortable, tastelessly furnished living-room in Luton and practise yawning with his mouth shut. He will be impervious to boredom. He will admire his prospect's tank of smelly goldfish and express enthusiasm for hearing details of the prospect's wife's recent operation for haemorrhoids.

I could no more sell life insurance than roller skate in a vat of peanut butter, but somebody's got to do it. Could it be you?

Why did I list expensive motorcars as an abstract? They're real aren't they? If you think about it for a moment they are a good deal more esoteric than you would at first assume. What the car salesman is really offering is 'life style', 'sexual charisma', 'status'. He, too, must understand a little about the human psyche. So many products are not simply the solid structure that constitute their physical being – they must be invested with 'personality', or, as my advertising chums would say, 'image'. No, it's not fanciful nonsense. With modern methods of research, design and manufacture, many products are virtually the same. What singles out the bestseller is how it is 'perceived' by the customers. This perception is critical, and the role of the salesman, whether through his company's advertising or through his own advocacy, is a major force in establishing this important lock on potential buyers' imaginations.

So, when choosing your field for a selling career, be prepared to use your intellectual skills and your ingenuity to create around your product a strong personality which has a chance of exciting your customers.

If you are naturally gregarious and, dare it be said, slightly 'up-market' in your own personal style, then fine art, real estate, airtime sales or antique furniture could be happy hunting grounds for you. On the other hand, however, you may be five feet three, running to fat, balding and fond of Margate. Do not despair. Such people usually end up selling rivets, paint, galvanized ladders and adhesives to do-it-yourself emporiums in the Loughborough area.

(An Old Etonian accent, suede shoes and a carnation in the buttonhole are not conducive to success in the building materials trade.)

Pick a product field that genuinely interests you. Be hot for knowledge. Absorb it. Eat it. Sleep it. Live it. Above all, *show* your enthusiasm for what you're selling. If *you* don't believe in it you can't expect anybody else to!

The most successful salespeople I know are totally absorbed by their work. Leisure time and selling time blur and overlap to such a degree that nobody can see the join. But a word of warning. Don't be a bore about your chosen field. Timing is all. If you're buying the prospect dinner in Paris and she happens to be blonde, delicious and gasping for your lewd embrace, this is *not* the time to whip out your corrugated roofing catalogue with revised price list. Be cool. And enthusiastic? Yes, it *is* possible. Learn to *shimmer* with suppressed excitement. It's a super trick if you can learn the technique. And it only works if your feelings are genuine. Even about corrugated roofing.

Perhaps the most important choice you will have to make when considering a sales career is whether you will sell to the *general public*, or to other *specialists* in your chosen field. This really is a major decision and one which, if wrongly taken, can stunt your progress for ever and a day.

So, ask yourself these questions.

Am I a man or woman of the people? Do I enjoy strolling around housing estates in Milton Keynes? Do I really care about understains on little Johnny's soccer pants? Could I conduct a fascinating two-hour conversation on the doorstep of a retired traffic warden in Barnsley? Do I laugh at *Blankety Blank* on television? And do I have difficulty with the long words on page three of the *Sun* newspaper?

If the answer is 'Yes' to all of these questions you should stick to a selling career that brings you into daily contact with 'ordinary' – or, as they are sometimes called, 'real' – people.

If, conversely, the above prospect causes your stomach to heave and sweat to break out on the palms of your hands . . . I have even worse news for you. Selling heavy engineering products to professional engineers is much more awful.

But you *must* choose. All right, I hear you mutter, those are two extreme cases. What about selling fine art? Lovely surroundings in Bond Street, velvet-covered walls, slim Chippendale chairs, a few Rembrandts hanging nonchalantly beneath glittering chandeliers. A glass of dry sherry with some erudite international collector, as he listens, absorbed, to your patter about early sixteenth-century Russian icons – and presto – an order for ten grand before lunch! Let me assure you that it is not a bit like that. The commercial reality of the high art business is pretty frightening. It's a cutthroat, dog-eat-dog game where only the fittest can possibly survive.

So how *do* you choose?

Write down the six things that interest you *most* in life. Do it quickly without hesitating too long. OK. Now cross out sex and drinking and that will leave you with four. It doesn't matter that you've written down golf, music, chess and the cinema. It's a start. Remember a *lifetime's* selling career is a hell of a long time and you might as well get into something that you like *instinctively*.

Work *outwards* from your four choices. If you do love golf, why not think about a career selling sports equipment? If you are turned on by music you could always start on the ladder of success and fulfilment by becoming a salesman in a musical instrument shop. You get the idea? Stay close to what gives *you* enjoyment. This will ensure that the enthusiasm you generate when you sell is genuine.

How often have you met a person who has a boring job (let's face it, *most* people have boring jobs), and this person only comes alive when you tackle him on his favourite hobby? The Jekyll and Hyde effect is startling. Take the tired, demoralized factory worker who loathes the production line but collects butterflies. The way to touch his life button is not to reminisce about rivet-packing machinery, but to ask him about some rare species of red admiral. Just think what could be achieved in that man's life if his hobby were his work. For the really successful salesman, his hobby *is* his work. Or at least a major part of it.

The big step in selecting the right sales career for you is overcoming that irrational dread that Englishmen have of being *too* pushy and *too* successful. The golf enthusiast, for example, is allowed to be enthusiastic as long as he remains strictly amateur.

You must bury those Anglo-Saxon inhibitions and say to yourself, I *love* golf – or tennis, or newt-sexing or ferret-strangling or whatever – and then trace your career outwards from that one burning point of interest.

Right. So you've made the two important decisions. You've chosen to sell direct to Joe Public, or not, as the case may be, and you've thought hard, and I mean really hard, about the handful of subjects that really whip your adrenaline into a frenzy.

Now you must jam your foot on the first rung of the ladder and get a job. Later on we'll examine the dos and don'ts of that *first interview for a sales job*.

If you are already involved in a selling career but seek a change of climate, the principles are the same. Selling *yourself*, which is what job interviews are all about, is the hardest pitch of all and one which requires great subtlety, deftness of touch and an almost mystical ability to tune into your future employer's vibrations. Still interested? Then read on. If not, there are plenty of good correspondence courses on accountancy and maggot farming.

3. Women in Sales

Do they have to try harder?
Is a pretty face enough to achieve success?
What about the male backlash?

As in most other walks of life, the female role has undergone a dramatic metamorphosis. Women now occupy a whole raft of positions in commerce, art and politics which would have been unthinkable even ten years ago.

Most men, if they are honest, feel uncomfortable, even threatened by the more vigorous activities of the Women's Liberation Movement. Our own ladies in this country, however, while vociferous, are pussycats compared to their sisters in the United States. Men are slowly learning to cope with this new pressure – but, like all social revolutions, there are inevitable casualties. On both sides.

But women as salespeople? Is it such a new idea? Surely we've had lady 'demonstrators' in department stores for years? And pretty young girls wearing coloured sashes acting as 'merchandisers' for new product launches or trade fairs?

All perfectly true – but using women in this way only enrages the more ambitious of them because it categorizes their ability within very narrow and very patronizing criteria. It's OK – the argument used to run – to hire women as demonstrators because they only need to look decorative and learn to repeat a few simple instructions. Much the same sort of attitude used to be applied to merchandisers. You have a new brand of aftershave to market? Why not send out a bevy of gorgeous young things in tight skirts to dazzle the retail trade whilst leaving the serious negotiating work to the Real Man?

No, it's not bullshit. That's how it used to be. And still *is* in some quarters.

But times they are a-changing. Many top marketing jobs are now filled by women and in the more progressive sales companies the women executives often outpace their male counterparts.

Is this the end of civilization as we know it? Should we chaps run howling and emasculated back to mummy and cry 'Foul!' Aren't women in sales 'taking' work away from more 'deserving' men? If you believe that, you're either an Australian or a wimp!

Prejudice still exists. Let's not be mealy-mouthed about this. *You're* prejudiced, aren't you? And I sure as hell am. There's no way we can slough off the indelible imprints of our cultural background, or the social conditioning we have been subjected to.

What we *have to do*, if we fancy the idea of survival, which I rather do, is to learn to live with the accelerating phenomenon of women in sales. And enjoy it. Because it's good news for *all* of us.

Before we explore why it's so good for us, let's look at a lighthearted table. Be *honest* with yourself and tick those items which are most like your *own* views on the subject.

Women make lousy salespeople because:	Women make great salespeople because:
They lack ambition	They need to 'overachieve'
They get monthly cramps	They have tidy minds
They get pregnant	They are more likely to understand the role of the consumer
They lack stamina	They smell nice
They have butterfly minds	They crave independence
They distract men from serious business	They're better organized

They ought to be at home cooking a nice meal	They simply want to contribute more to the family budget
They take jobs away from the boys	They don't get drunk and skulk in the office hungover and unshaven

Well, do women try harder? In my experience the answer has to be 'yes'.

Given that you have two candidates of equal ability and your selection process is sound, you will find that the woman will feel the need to perform well *in order to overcome what she perceives as a handicap at the starting gate*. A handicap at the starting gate? Yes, selling is *still* a largely male preserve and a woman can never afford to coast. Any deviation, however temporary, from the highest standards *can* result in the men nudging each other and saying, 'What do you expect? She's neurotic/It's her period/Her boyfriend's ditched her/She's only here till she catches a husband.' And so on. We've all heard it.

So, the dedicated woman in sales *knows* that she will be judged in a slightly different light from her male colleagues. Hence the obsession women high-fliers have with overachieving.

And even today the odds are stacked against them. If they are too 'feminine' they will be accused of being soft, yielding, using their charms or their bodies or both to confuse and deceive the old pressurized male.

If they bottle down their emotions and eschew 'femininity' by, say, adopting a severe hairstyle, no make-up and a *tough* persona, etc., they run the risk of being labelled 'old trouts', 'ice maidens', or 'professional virgins'. And these are some of the more polite epithets.

But there are many women who have scaled the heights and achieved success without becoming stereotypes. It's not only possible to be successful, tough and *feminine*, it's perfectly *natural*.

> Don't men ever cry?
> Or cuddle their children?
> Or daydream about their lovers?
> Or have 'bad days' when they snarl and sulk?

Oh yes they bloody well do.

Now, let me make something quite plain. I am not an uncritical, fawning admirer of the Women's Liberation Movement – at least in its more virulent manifestations. I am, because of my background and experience, very much like your average bloke. A bit chauvinistic. Specially when there are no women about. I react to women in a *primeval* way. That is to say I find the physical and psychological differences between the sexes *impossible* to ignore. So do most men.

And, like most men, I observe the changes that have taken place in the male/female relationship with a mixture of admiration and unease.

This said, what advice can be offered to the woman who wants to make a career in sales?

.Fundamentally, her approach should be the same as her masculine counterpart. She must be *fired* with ambition and *hungry* to succeed; she must possess an *inner* toughness – which, incidentally, is infinitely more valuable than a shallow, outer toughness – and be prepared to work long and hard to achieve her goals.

And what about her 'femaleness'? Should it be consciously exploited or discreetly suppressed? Neither, actually. That she is a woman is simply a matter of fact, like having red hair or being tall or short or extrovert or shy. What she *should* exploit are her positive qualities which transcend gender.

We've heard about her *disadvantages*, whether real or imagined. What natural advantages does she have over the male? Views will differ, but my checklist is as follows.

A woman in sales is still in a *minority position*. This gives her a unique value and 'high visibility'. Women, in my experience, are better at *detailed* planning than men. (All that inherited skill in balancing family budgets, producing three-course meals from two cold chops and half a potato, managing children, placating elder brothers.)

Women as *consumers* are still the primary target audience for most mass advertisers. Thus, they tend to have real 'sharp-end' experience of making twenty quid go a long way in Tesco's. They are often *natural* money managers. They understand, in a basic, common-sense way, the importance of cash flow and forward budgeting.

Women making a sales pitch seem to be possessed of more credibility than some men. I don't wish to make too much of this, but ask yourself the following question – how many spivvy, foot-in-the-door sales*women* have you encountered?

Finally, and perhaps surprisingly, women have more *tenacity* than they are given credit for.

With all these built-in advantages, is it any wonder that the female salestar is a growing factor in our commercial life?

But it's not·all plain sailing for the golden girl with the Gucci scarf, pigskin briefcase and Chanel No. 5, as she plans her journey into the competitive selling jungle. Dangerous traps await her. Some of them human. And male. Here are just a few obstacles she will have to face – which no man ever has to contemplate.

If she's passably presentable she will have to cope with a fair amount of *mild* sexual intimidation. The male buyer in many trades may well parade his prejudices openly; the girlie calendar conspicuously displayed on the office wall, the subtle innuendo, the wink, the nudge-nudge attempt at establishing his macho image.

Most smart saleswomen can take these things in their stride. The important thing is *not to rise to the bait*. Men *hate* being put down – particularly by a person of the opposite sex – but sometimes it *has* to be done in order to stabilize a sales relationship.

I know a very talented saleswoman who was pitching to an excessively hostile buyer. He could sense that this lady was a good deal smarter than he was and in order to re-establish what he thought was his 'natural' initiative he tried shock tactics.

'Ever screwed a Chinaman?' he suddenly asked. The lady smiled gracefully and shook her head.

'As a matter of fact, no. Why? Have you?'

It must also be said that there are still many women who *resent their more talented sisters in business*. Far from rejoicing in the progress of women as sales executives, they display jealousy and bitterness. We've all met the disillusioned housewife who is bored with her domestic role and three whining children and who is overtly hostile towards the talented businesswoman she meets at a party.

For some women, sadly, the stifling restrictions of their own environment cause them to mistrust others who have broken out of the stereotyped mould. But there are countless women who have combined both domestic and professional roles with impunity. It *can* be done provided there exists the *will* for it to be achieved. And maybe an understanding bloke or two in the background. Or no bloke at all. As the case may be.

Women in sales come in as many shapes and sizes as their male counterparts, but in order to help identify the two main types – as we did with the men (tigers and foxes) – we'll call them *tigresses* and *vixens*.

Tigresses are those fortunate ladies who possess both high-octane sexuality (never to be underestimated, even in these liberated days) and a genuine flair for business.

The vixens, on the other hand, are usually brilliant intellectually, and determined to win by exclusively cerebral means. They are not necessarily *plain*, but they do reject sex appeal as an ingredient in their *business lives*. Sometimes in vain.

Anna Ford, the broadcaster, once complained of 'body fascism' because men's initial reaction was always to her looks rather than her ability. I have never known what she was complaining about. I would have thought she was twice blessed. Or would she rather have been ugly?

Dangerous though broad generalizations are, here is my checklist to help identify the two main types.

Tigresses

Tall, slim, sexually magnetic, volatile, extrovert

Fashionably dressed (tailored suits, silk blouses, very high heels, expensive perfume, stunning hairstyle)

Not usually from the upper classes (the accent is *too* Princess Anne)

Sociable, loves theatre, music, top restaurants

Drives fast, diets, plays tennis, skis, swims

Has lovers, but is always in charge, calling the shots

Will age magnificently (tigresses have great bone structure)

No children unless looked after by a nanny

Aggressive presenter

Highly theatrical

Vixens

High academic qualifications (Honours degree in economics)

Shortish, plays *down* appearance (rarely uses make-up)

Wears good but inexpensive clothes, rarely puts on high heels, except *formally*

Reads avidly, listens to music, but hates 'pop'

Prefers cooking at home to visiting restaurants

Writes lucidly and is fanatical about research

Obstinate, argues patiently, winning by slow persuasion, underlined by *faint* regional accent

Shuns conventions, dislikes appearing on conference platforms

Drives plain car, slowly

Is married or monogamous

Male partner usually dull, but supportive

Will run to fat in middle age

Best in one-to-one sales situations

Tigresses can be found in advertising, fashion, cosmetics and the music business. They *revel* in the admiring glances their glossy appearance projects. They can be bitchy, even harsh, and they do not suffer fools gladly.

They tend to speak quickly, firing off sentences with machine-gun rapidity, and they inject the occasional swearword into their dialogue. It's usually a real shocker, too. This still throws some men off balance, particularly in places like Bootle where men are men and women should be in curlers or behind the bar of 'The Wart and Ferret'.

Tigresses enjoy sex. They have been having multiple orgasms since they were seventeen. Their liaisons tend to be uninhibited and they are very skilled in bed. This doesn't prevent them from telling their men what they *want* – in colourful and precise detail. ('I said *bigger* circles, Gerald – oooh, that's good.' And Gerald, who is often ten years younger than his tigress, doesn't mind at all. In fact, it excites the hell out of him.)

Tigresses are excellent presenters; they possess *natural* acting ability and a fine sense of timing. They enjoy outstaring men across large desks and lighting their own cigarettes with solid gold Cartier lighters. They look good in expensive restaurants and waiters fawn over them.

They read the *Guardian* but disagree with most of its views, especially those espoused on the Women's Page. They are closet readers of *Cosmopolitan* and the occasional Judith Krantz novel.

They wear outrageous underwear, particularly on those days when business calls for a severe black suit, white satin blouse and patent leather shoes.

They will claw and manoeuvre their way to the top – and stay there.

Only very special men can endure being married to them, even though dozens of their ex-beaux still profess undying love.

They are growing in number and are a force to be reckoned with.

Vixens, on the other hand, succeed *in spite of* their other commitments and interests. They are in research, computers, light engineering, pharmaceutical marketing and life insurance.

Often they have husbands working as software specialists in Slough who are devoted fathers and frequently put the kids to bed before their vixens get home.

They are exceptionally *clever* women, with a huge capacity for absorbing detail. They will read research reports under the drier at their local hairdresser when other women are gossiping.

They make up in *tenacity* what they lack in charisma. They are not as streetwise as their tigress sisters, and if a client propositions them in a restaurant they probably won't notice.

They don't French kiss; it's untidy. (Their husbands, who are invariably balding, agree.) Sex is OK. But messy.

Vixens are closet *Woman's Own* readers. And they are good but unspectacular cooks.

They can argue patiently with a client until he is stunned into saying 'yes' by the sheer tedium of their logic. When vixens are angry, they sound like their mothers, and their accents slip displaying the sounds of the Midlands.

They are exceedingly well organized and need very little sleep. They work on trains and aeroplanes and have been known to take Government White Papers on holiday to Majorca with them.

Their children are clever – and well behaved. (Unlike the tigress's kids, *if* she has any, who snort coke and fornicate with their yoga teachers.)

They are a substantial influence in the more sober trades and professions.

They do not fear middle age – secretly longing to enjoy chocolate gateaux and marzipan and wear more *sensible* clothes.

They make good bosses. But will disapprove of 'flashy' men to whom they feel intellectually superior.

The *vixens* are here to stay.

So are the *tigresses*. And we men will have to watch our flanks!

4. The Importance of Speech Patterns

Talk proper and don't mumble like an oaf

WARNING   A number of statements in this chapter will give offence to some readers. I make no apology. If people choose to be insulted, even mildly, let them rest assured in the knowledge that the *insult was intended*, and this is no time to be mealy-mouthed. I have always admired the truly *well-aimed* and *deeply wounding* insult as being infinitely preferable to the more insipid *accidental* slight which is on the whole rather wet.

Fine. Decks cleared now? Sensitivities primed? Let us proceed. Speech is important to the successful salesman, and *good* speech even *more* important. Without a decent vocabulary, life can be an uphill struggle.

Tone of voice is perhaps the real key to persuasive communication (always assuming of course that *what* is actually said makes sense). An *over-loud* delivery is counterproductive – most customers object to the salesmanship-by-megaphone technique and the temptation to bellow usually indicates the threadbare nature of the case being presented.

Speaking clearly, however, is so obvious a virtue as to need no further illumination. If you have ever stood in Soho's Berwick Market and listened to the street-traders you will most certainly have observed that, however rough their vocabulary, their articulation is razor sharp. They don't want a word of their pitch to be misheard and neither should you.

The *softly spoken* salesman, alas, must also beware – the

scarcely audible monologue suggests not only lack of confidence but a rare and highly contagious throat disease too awful to contemplate. Apart from which, most clients loathe having to ask you to repeat everything twice.

So don't mumble. It's such an unattractive trait. Leave that to Gregorian monks, employees of British Telecom and surly waiters at London Airport cafeterias.

Don't *gabble*. This was something I used to be guilty of during my tinned food days in London's East End. A torrent of words, I discovered, only served to blur my otherwise compelling message about the efficiency of the baked bean as a nutritious snackette. Discipline yourself with iron ruthlessness, therefore, to deliver the chosen words at a reasonable clip.

Accents

This is the insulting bit so hang on to your hats. If you are the unfortunate possessor of a strong – and I mean *strong* – Lancashire, Yorkshire, Birmingham or Liverpool accent you should only embark on a sales career if:

(a) You remain in your own region among people who speak as hideously as you.
(b) You hire a speech therapist and pay him handsomely to eradicate all those nerve-grating vowels and aggressive diphthongs.
(c) You resolve to use only non-verbal means of communication – like semaphore.
(d) You engage the services of a ventriloquist.

No, I'm afraid I'm not prepared to soften the blow. All this loose talk about a Yorkshire accent being 'honest and gritty' is sheer twaddle. It's just ugly. The Birmingham or Brummy accent is so mournful and grotesque that it should be punishable by the full rigour of the law. Likewise

Liverpudlian and Geordie, both in their *extreme* manifestations deeply offensive to the ear.

How often in my youth have I chanced upon a delectable young goddess with shining hair and a trim figure only to experience my lust transformed to ashes when she opened her mouth and uttered?

Well, never actually, but you know what I mean. Having stated earlier that I would declare myself in this chapter with such unvarnished frankness as to be positively insulting to some readers, I now, cravenly and without shame, *dilute* and *qualify* my previous remarks. But not much – so you can wipe that smile off your face, wack!

If the aforementioned are *mild*, i.e., tempered by the soothing sounds of the south, they can – by a process of cunning metamorphosis – become positively attractive. A *hint* of northern grit is OK. But let's not tear the arse out of it, *please*.

Do I feel the same about the naked coarseness of an East End cockney accent? Yes, I do. Colourful it may be for comedians and taxi drivers, but it is not the accent for the truly aspiring salestar. With one notable exception. If your dad has a pitch in Petticoat Lane and you are to follow his footsteps flogging nylon shirts and digital watches, impervious to extremes in temperature at depths of eight million fathoms (the watches, not the shirts), then the cockney-style delivery becomes a badge of pride. Unfortunately, career openings in Petticoat Lane and Berwick Market are somewhat limited and the rewards exaggerated.

If, all the above notwithstanding, you are lucky enough to speak with a *gentle* Scottish burr (not broken-glass Gorbals), a *soft* Irish lilt or any of the warm West Country brogues, you are among Nature's chosen salespeople.

How about BBC 'Standard' English? Am I suggesting all salesmen and women should emulate Richard Baker and Angela Rippon? No, I am not suggesting that at all – although both Baker and Rippon do speak rather well. What I am suggesting is that you should iron out the ugly bits in your voice and practise diction with the same dedication as Rudolph Nureyev studied the writhing leap with sprayed-on white jockstrap.

Surprisingly perhaps, the over-refined public school accent can, in this day and age, be as much of a handicap as that of a rasping yobbo. Exceptions to this dictum however might be the salesmen in Sotheby's who all sound like the offspring of Royal dukes. Do not be deceived by the subtle drawl of motor-showroom representatives. They are only *imitating* a public school accent, as you will discover if you make them say 'now' or 'how'. These words will emerge as 'neow' and 'heow' in what has become standard Edward Heath.

The purchase of a simple tape-recorder with microphone attachment is all you need if you are to turn your present shambling, high-pitched drivel into words of riveting conviction. Most of us don't *hear* our own voices in the same way others do, and it usually comes as a nasty shock when we first experience it.

It's time for another table:

'Good' accents	Not so good accents
Plain English – southern style	'Extreme' public school
Scots	Yorkshire
Irish	Lancashire
Bostonian American (but only if you were born in Neasden)	Birmingham
	Liverpool
	Cockney
Wiltshire	Mock West Indian ('You dig man!')
Hampshire	
Devon	
Cornwall	
Somerset	
Dorset	

No, I haven't forgotten the Welsh. Welsh is not an accent, it's a foreign language – even when it's spoken in English. The best advice I can therefore offer to Welsh readers is, if you want to become a sales superstar try *singing* your message. At least you will be unlikely to fall into the trap of your English cousins who insist on inserting the words 'you know' or 'like' into all their sentences.

5. The Trappings of Success

Is a gold Rolex over the top?

Should I look less affluent than my customers?

People called Stan don't drink Château-Lafite Rothschild '74

A brilliant salesman that I know owns a Bentley and a dozen superb Savile Row suits. He is in the real estate business and deals in large sums of money at a very high level. In his case his clients *expect* him to display the badges of wealth – indeed they bask in his reflected affluence. Their reasoning is simple: if they are to commit a million pounds of corporate funds on a building or real estate project they want to be reassured that they are dealing with a man who is not overawed by a string of noughts on a balance sheet.

In many trades, however, it is the kiss of death to display a life style that upstages your customer's. Well, are there any guidelines? Apart from common sense? Here's my own checklist.

It's OK to strut your stuff (gold cufflinks, eight-cylinder car, nine-inch cigars, crocodile-skin briefcase, etc.) *only* if:

(a) Your client is very rich himself personally.
(b) You are in a 'high profile' trade like real estate, fine art, bloodstock sales, diamonds or movie broking.
(c) You are not under thirty. (Clients – most of them anyway – think rewards should accrue 'over time'. Too much, too soon, gets right up their noses.)
(d) You actually *own* your company. If you're the boss, they'll *have* to take you on face value.

On the other hand it is wiser to leave the shiny red Ferrari behind, if:

(a) Your client's headquarters are in the middle of a trading estate in a depressed part of Huddersfield.
(b) The decision-maker you know you have to deal with is not the possessor of a company car himself.
(c) The firm you call on is, to your knowledge, either laying off staff or suffering from a trade shortfall. (The sight of you poncing up in a vicuña coat behind the wheel of a twenty-grand car will be about as welcome as a turd in a swimming pool.)

Here are some more quick tips.

If you get talking about *salaries* and your client reveals that he is earning five thousand a year less than you are – *shut up*. Clients hate their suppliers being paid more than they are.

It's OK to hint at big mortgage commitments and rolling Barclaycard debts – salesmen are expected to live beyond their means. Knowing that the salesman is on a treadmill of extended credit gives the client a warm, sticky feeling in his lower abdomen. If he *knows* you're in debt he'll almost forgive the four-grand gold Rolex Oyster. But you should not, on the other hand, convey *desperate and uncontrolled impecuniousness*. This will convince the client that you are a foolish little twit who is all mouth and no trousers.

The degree of affluence that can be exhibited therefore will be determined by the *nature of your business* (funeral directors don't prance about in white Gucci shoes) and the circumstances of the client within that business.

I once asked a rich advertising agent if he always drove in his apple-green Rolls-Royce when visiting clients (most of whom he could have bought with his small change). He pondered for a moment and then said, 'If I discern that it might be a problem, I instruct my chauffeur *not* to clean the car that day.' But he was in a jesting mood. I think.

The manifestations of success can sometimes spill over in

unexpected ways and in unexpected circumstances. In certain trades, the business lunch has the importance of a tribal ritual. It is also an act of comradeship, an economic ego-display or an act of subtle intimidation. An aspiring salesman who takes a client to a restaurant that is *too rich in its trappings and style* for the status of that client is playing with fire.

So, if you are flogging a device that unblocks drains to the deputy assistant sanitary engineer of Slagthorpe City Council, it will do you precious little good to drag him into the Grand Snobbo Grill Room for lunch and try to impress him with your knowledge of French wines. He will, in most cases, feel *threatened* rather than flattered and you will find him self-consciously fingering his threadbare cuffs while he watches neighbouring diners gorging themselves on duck *à l'orange* and caviare. Better by far to take him to a good pub with a decent restaurant and let him relax.

You can reverse the situation too. A client who is known to be a *bon viveur* and lover of elegant restaurants will not warm to you if you stick a pork pie and a pint of brown and mild under his nose.

Personally, I find pubs impossible to do business in, and, on those rare occasions that I do find an advertising agency executive with modest tastes, I prefer the atmosphere of a good wine bar.

If a client takes *you* to lunch – then *wherever he takes you is absolutely OK*. Have you got that?

Even if it's Percy's Copper Kettle Café on that noisy bit of the A308?

Yes, even if it's Percy's Copper Kettle Café on that *deafening* bit of the A308. You will *eat* those greasy chips and compliment him on his choice of Tizer with which the rissoles will be washed down.

Why?

Well, it could be a test. I once had a client who deliberately bought me vile meals. He was just longing for me to throw up or hurl the plate of tripe and parsnips out of the window.

I never gave him the satisfaction. Admittedly, this was years ago, when there were no middle-range restaurants in London – it was either the Savoy Grill or Ned's Oily Spoon. These days, with such a cornucopia of choice, nobody has any excuse for getting it wrong.

Isn't all this business of restaurants a bit of peripheral nonsense? Is it *really* so important? The answer is yes, if *your* trade is the kind of trade that expects entertainment of a certain standard.

If all else fails, I have found a plate of sandwiches in the office with a client (real plates, please, no plastic junk) can work wonders.

Just remember, every punter is different and people called Stan don't drink Château-Lafite Rothschild '74.

6. The Job Interview
Don't forget to do your homework
Is there such a thing as too much self-confidence?

'It is not unreasonable to assume that an aspiring salesman or woman will perform better at a job interview than a non-salesperson.' True or false?

False.

Interviews are usually artificial set pieces where both interviewer and interviewee are on 'special' behaviour, designed to mask their true identities and create an overall impression of smooth omnipotence.

I wish somebody could invent an acceptable alternative to the unnatural tyranny of the job interview. Until somebody does, however, you'll just have to grit your teeth and make the best of it.

If you are applying for a sales job, it is worth remembering that the most important commodity you will *ever* have to sell is *yourself*. Even after you've secured the job of your choice, the 'self-promotion' must continue, probably until the day you either retire, or drop dead from frustration in front of that old fart of a buyer, Mr Lumpfuttock of Slough.

So, whereas your common-or-garden architect, draughtsman, noodle-taster or brain surgeon may be forgiven if he fumbles his job interview, *you* – the person who intends to take up persuasion *for a living* – must always be judged by much harsher criteria.

After all, the brain surgeon can't actually demonstrate his precise techniques in front of the chief of the hospital medical staff's selection committee, but *you* can. You have to sell *yourself*. And how.

So, first and foremost, let's glance at another checklist:

Before the interview

1. Find out and *remember* as much as you can about the company and its products.
2. Get a copy of its last annual report and study the *bottom line*. Memorize its pre- and post-tax profits.
3. If it's feasible, buy and try one of the company's products (unless it's racing yachts or intercontinental ballistic missiles).
4. Try and get a fix on how the company's customers judge it. If they're in retail, go and ask a shopkeeper about their range. You'll be surprised how helpful this ruse can be. It also impresses the ass off an interviewer when you reveal you've conducted this research.
5. Try and talk to one of the company's sales force beforehand. If he/she looks glum or shifty, you may be leaping into a quagmire. Salespeople should *radiate* enthusiasm, remember.
6. If the company is a prominent advertiser, *form your own opinion* about its press or TV campaign and be ready to offer that opinion . . . but with discretion. ('I think your ads stink' is not a shrewd tactic.)
7. Try and rehearse a *plausible* reason or reasons why the company should offer you a job. But, remember, go steady on the ego trip. 'Because I'm Mr Wonderful' is not enough to land that key position you have long lusted after. Whatever reason or reasons you *do* give should always contain an element of 'customer-benefit' too. 'Because I'm fascinated by your product range *and* I believe I can develop its penetration in the untapped Wigan hinterlands.' Provided the hinterlands of Wigan are accepted as being untapped, of course.

    You will have researched this beforehand, won't you?

How about appearance?

Clearly, you should want to look your best at a job interview, but be careful. Don't overdress yourself so that you look like a refugee from an Aztec funeral.

If you don't normally wear a carnation in your buttonhole or a Chinese silk waistcoat, *don't* put them on just for the interview. Even if you borrowed them from your dad. Salesmen are expected to look crisp and tidy – more so than in many other professions – and a little attention to detail beforehand can reap substantial dividends.

You *don't* need to be expensively dressed to create the right impression, but an untidily clad salesman suggests that the sloppiness may be carried through into his work. Dressing well is a compliment to the people who have to look at you all day, and – in spite of the more relaxed sartorial standards of the 1980s – it still remains important for a salesman or woman to present themselves well.

Not so long ago representatives working for the great grocery manufacturing companies were *required* to wear striped trousers and black coats. Even as a young representative selling space for the now-defunct *Daily Herald* newspaper, I was instructed always to wear a *dark* suit and a white or cream shirt. Striped or coloured shirts were frowned upon as being 'flippant'!

As were salesmen who went around bare-headed. I personally loathe hats. They make me look like a bailiff or an out-of-work funeral director, but in the 1950s headgear was essential. My sales manager was shocked when he spotted me walking along The Strand without a hat. 'You might have met a client,' he explained sternly, 'and you would have had *nothing* to raise in greeting!'

Fortunately, the stuffy rigidity of those days has now gone and people can express more of their own personalities in the way they dress.

The suit – dare I say it – is still about the most practical outfit a salesman can choose. He can indulge his flair for silk shirts, Italian ties and expensive shoes if he wants to, but still look *businesslike*.

Watch the more *personal* areas too. Like fingernails and hair. Salesmen use their hands a lot, gesticulating, pointing at price lists, checking stock levels in retail stores. Grubby fingernails or hideous nicotine stains are a major no-no. So stop nibbling at your thumbnail, you neurotic little fool!

Hair: long is OK. Short is OK. Dirty isn't. Believe it, or believe it not, I was once visited by a central heating salesman whose personal appearance was a disgrace. Frayed cuffs, muddy shoes, gravy stains on the tie. But worse! During his sales pitch, something small and horrid crawled out of his hair and scuttled across his left ear. My attention to his sales monologue dwindled like snow on a stove.

When you eventually find yourself sitting down in somebody's office actually being interviewed, try to ascertain *early on* whether the man/woman you are facing is a 'listener' or a 'talker'. In theory, at least, *you* the interviewee should do most of the talking. It's *you* who they want to hear about, isn't it? Well, not always.

If you realize you are in the presence of a congenital 'talker' who rabbits on about his 'great company' and its 'dynamic corporate spirit' and other flatulent guff, you'll just have to listen. Look intelligent. Stifle the urge to yawn, or urinate discreetly over his carpet, and compose your features for a *long, boring session*.

Quite often 'talker interviewers' will warm to you without you as much as uttering a syllable. At the end of a twenty-minute monologue they will leap up, grab you by the hand and exclaim, 'It's been *marvellous* talking to you – I'm *sure* you'll fit into our team.'

If you fancy the job, don't disillusion them. Raise your price by about a grand a year. The chances are they'll buy you anyway. If you *don't* want the job, all you've lost then is twenty minutes of your life. You can spare *that*, can't you?

Above all, at an interview, *be alive*. There's nothing worse than trying to talk with 180 pounds' worth of inanimate human spam.

And *sell* yourself. Smile. Respond. Move. Gesticulate – but sparingly. Trot out the skein of knowledge you have painstakingly absorbed about the company, and make sure you *ask questions too*. There's nothing an interviewer likes more than being treated like an all-seeing, all-knowing oracle.

Beware of trick questions, like, 'Do you think Mr Wedgwood-Benn would be good or bad for British business if he became Chancellor of the Exchequer?' The sales director of the company *might* be a member of the Militant Tendency. Or the Monday Club.

Either way, whatever answer you give won't be the right one. Avoid 'hyping' your personal interests and hobbies. *Nobody* believes application forms which glibly state, 'My interests are antique collecting, hang-gliding, oil painting, tennis, chess, underwater judo, brass rubbing, exorcism, and creating Nazi recipes for diabetics.'

And don't lie about your past. If you spent three months in Rekjavik shampooing albino llamas for a private zoo, for God's sake *admit* it. Come to think of it, if you *did* spend three months in Rekjavik shampooing albino llamas, make sure it's the *first* thing you write on your application form. And don't be afraid to own up to periods of unemployment. It's no disgrace these days.

Above all, keep selling yourself. You have a limited shelf life, remember, and you need to maximize your potential before your teeth drop out.

Never argue at a job interview, however tempting it may be. Even if you've decided the job definitely isn't for you, *still don't argue*. Try and quit early and move on to the next interview.

What's a job worth – and how much should you ask for at an interview?

Personally, I wouldn't trust a company who asks an interviewee, 'Well, how much do *you* think the job is worth, Mr Turner?'

They should know that, damn them! What are they trying to do – get you on the cheap?

If you have been diligent in your pre-interview research, and assuming no job-price has been indicated already, you can be in possession of that information *before* you sit down in the personnel director's tastefully furnished office overlooking the offal-crushing plant which has been laid out like an Italian Renaissance garden or Jewish cemetery.

If you *know* that the going rate for the job you are applying for is £10,000 – and you've got all the necessary experience and qualifications – ask for £11,000. If you are a newcomer, in need of training and with very limited experience, you will, of course, be on less positive ground.

The golden rule, however, is to avoid working for a company who thinks salesmen should be *cheap*. In any organization that needs to market its wares in a highly competitive and volatile world, the sales force should be the high-fliers as far as earnings are concerned. Selling yourself, as I have indicated before, is the cornerstone of any interview, and you *must* place a value on your services. Of course, you may have to negotiate – that's normal – but don't be browbeaten.

You can learn a lot at the interview by studying the interviewer, particularly if he is the sales director or sales manager. That could be *you* in a few years' time. Is the man opposite the sort of person you want to become? Is he fat, greasy, shabbily dressed? Does he roll his own cheap cigarettes and keep a bottle of sweet sherry prominently displayed on his formica-topped sideboard?

Or does he exude a successful ambience? Wear classy shoes? Do his personal vibes spell 'money' and 'dynamism'?

These are not trivial considerations. You don't want to work for a jerk, do you?

Avoid accepting employment offers from men who wear hats in the office. Or men who don't look you in the eye when they talk. Or men who wear cardigans under their suits or little tin badges on their lapels. Scientific research of a staggering complexity has conclusively determined that such men are absolute prats.

Men who get up from behind their desks and pace about while they interview you fall into two categories. Either they are genuine enthusiasts who are fired up with the excitement of talking about work. If so, you'll *know* because it *shows*. Or they will be jittery no-hopers with dyspepsia who are trying to shake down a too-large helping of soggy apple crumble from the staff canteen.

One of the best pointers you can obtain as to whether the sales function in a company is highly regarded or not is to see the sales director *with his managing director*.

Good signs to watch for are an easy respect between the two of them, a natural harmony which is essential for business, and a complete absence of grovelling, forelock-pulling or excessive formality.

Bad signs are twitching, sudden sweating, icy politeness, and phrases like, 'Oh, indubitably, Mr Vole-strangler . . .', 'If I may be so bold, Mr Volestrangler . . .', 'And how are Mrs Volestrangler's warts responding to treatment, sir?'

Remember, interviews are a two-way communication and the interviewer as well as the interviewee should be putting his best foot forward. You will be making a grave mistake if you accept employment with a company whose senior management lack conviction or enthusiasm, and *the ability to communicate it*.

If the man or woman who interviews you is younger than you are – rejoice. This is usually a good sign. Unless you happen to be seventy-four next birthday and are applying for a rep's job with a sporting goods manufacturer. Young bosses are more likely to be flexible and imaginative, and they are less likely to be soured by years of frustration or thwarted ambition. In my experience, young executives help keep their older colleagues young, too.

Above all, don't forget one of the fundamental principles of selling. You have to demonstrate good reasons and strong benefits to the employer if he takes you on. Make sure you have identified and mentally rehearsed at least *three* benefits that might accrue to the interviewer's organization should they be far-sighted enough to offer you a job.

Isn't offering a prospective employer a *benefit* a trifle patronizing? Won't he react sharply to such obvious blandishments? Well, yes he will if it's *obvious*.

But – make no mistake about this – unless you *can* identify some positive benefits why should he hire you in the first place? The colour of your eyes? The fact that you speak without dropping your aitches? You'll have to do better than that. Don't leave it to chance. *Sell* him a package of benefits.

He should hire you because:

You have already demonstrated an interest and real *enthusiasm* for his company.

You have laid out an impressive track record of your previous sales successes.

You *live* for your work.

You have declared a *determination* to succeed.

You can increase his company's sales.

You can respond to a challenge and you're a *fast* learner.

You want *his* job eventually. At least.

You *know* you are the best thing since sliced bread.

When the interview is finally complete, shake hands firmly, and if you genuinely want the job let that be the last thought you leave with the interviewer.

'Well, thank you, Mr McAlpine. I have really enjoyed talking to you about consolidated meat extracts. I feel even more enthusiastic than ever about joining your sales team – and I look forward to hearing from you.' And exit briskly.

Never shuffle out like a condom salesman at the Vatican. Even your departure must be stylish. And smile at his secretary and/or receptionist on the way to the lift. Many a confused personnel officer has been swayed by his secretary saying – minutes after the interviewee has left – 'Such a *nice* man. And such a *dazzling* smile.'

You'd better believe it. Not all personnel selection is scientific – even today. The human factor still counts for a lot.

7. 'He who hoots with the owls at night, cannot fly with the eagles at dawn'
Old Sioux Proverb

This will be the shortest chapter in the book – but read it carefully. If you're going to succeed as a salesman you will have to forget the conventional concept of normal working hours. Huge salaries and fat commissions are not earned by nine-to-fivers or beady-eyed clock-watchers.

Long hours require both mental and physical stamina – and it is the latter that many aspiring salestars woefully neglect. To maintain a sharp mind and a persuasive style means being alert to the vehicle that will always be more important to you than even a Rolls-Royce Corniche.

Your own body.

OK. Not everyone is a keep-fit fanatic. Blubbery out-of-condition salesmen do exist. But is that what you really want to be? Some people are born with constitutions that can withstand the abuses of too much food, too much drink, too little sleep and virtually no exercise. They are lucky. And rare.

Winston Churchill was one of these people. He was permanently overweight, drank heavily, smoked several of his famous cigars each day, and probably never broke into a run during the last fifty years of his life.

Most of us aren't like Winston Churchill. If we stuff ourselves with rich food and swallow brandy by the half pint, we'll almost certainly shorten our lifespan. But, perhaps more importantly, we will drastically lower our sales performance. The temptation to overindulge is prevalent amongst salespeople. The expense-account lunch; dinner with a client in a foreign country; the cocktail hour; a tray of processed airline food during a long flight; a hunk of fruitcake while working late at home on next month's sales forecasts; that extra nightcap you don't really need. I'm not suggesting you become an Olympic athlete overnight. Or an abstemious monk. But moderation is the watchword. In my experience too much booze can destroy a promising sales career.

Good salesmen are often gregarious, sociable fellows but it's tragic when a potential high-flier develops too keen a taste for the hard stuff. Apart from which, nobody loves a lush who can't function properly beyond midday because of his destructive drinking habits. Other staff resent it, respect is lost, and all too often a good man ends up on the skids.

I warn all my salespeople that boozers have no future in the team. Drink socially by all means. But stay sharp. Especially in the afternoon. And if the client insists on getting smashed, let him. It's his liver, not yours.

So, how do you stay fit? And how fit should you be? Well, there's no standard formula because we are all very different. But a little research into your own body condition will give you a few sure hints.

Ask yourself these questions.

Do I play a sport regularly?
Do I jog?
Do I exercise at home?
Do I sleep well?
Am I ashamed of my naked body when I see it *unexpectedly* in a mirror?
Am I overindulging in food and drink?

My own doctor says that 'being out of breath once a day' is a good rule to follow. Not gasping like a stranded fish – just breathing deeply *as a result of steady exercise*. The heart quickens and flushes the system with blood and oxygen. The lungs work like bellows, blowing away all the cobwebs and there follows a splendid feeling of wellbeing.

I have an exercise bicycle in my bedroom and religiously pedal it each morning for *five minutes only*. It's not onerous, it's pleasant. I feel my heart and lungs respond and I *know* it's doing me good. I also play tennis, ride and ski – regularly.

So get yourself a *routine* that suits your own life style and stick with it. You don't have to surrender to middle age and turn into a bladder of lard. Pull yourself together. Staying in shape will be a *positive* aid to selling. And your sex life will improve too. Which is very good news because regular sex is a splendid form of exercise in its own right. But not on a full stomach.

How much sleep should you get? As much as you *feel* you need. I like six or seven hours regularly and I feel trashy if I have too many very late nights. Nothing is more uncompelling than a bleary-eyed salesman who yawns in the middle of his pitch. Recently, a bunch of American doctors claimed we don't really need sleep at all. They said it was no more than an ingrained habit left over from the Stone Age when darkness made activity impossible, so men hunkered down in their pitch black caves until dawn. The doctors were talking crap. Have *you* ever tried *not* sleeping for a week?

There's only one thing worse than too little sleep – and that's *too much*. You can't store sleep, and staying in your crumpled pit until 11 a.m. on a Saturday will make you feel sluggish and possibly more tired than if you had leapt out from between the sheets at seven o'clock.

The old Red Indian proverb is worth remembering, even though all of us are guilty of overdoing things from time to time.

He who hoots with the owls at night
Cannot fly with the eagles at dawn.

And you want to be an eagle, don't you?

8. Getting Organized
Journey planning, keeping records and other grindingly boring necessities

We have all encountered the salesman who falls out of bed at 11 o'clock in the morning, slips on something casual, and arrives in the pub at opening time where a man in a camelhair coat and long side-whiskers is just longing to buy – for hard cash – whatever it is our hero is supposed to be selling.

In the harsh world that you and I inhabit such perfect opportunities exist only in the imagination. Leaving things to chance, basing your future prosperity on the 'big hit' or the 'ultimate deal', is rather like hoping for a pools win. It is very stupid.

Time is a highly perishable commodity and the serious salesman must learn to consume it profitably. No buyer respects a salesman who is a time-waster. And no salesman who is a congenital time-waster himself will ever get very far.

So, get that carcass of yours *out of bed* early and plan your day, your week, your month. Make it a discipline, like regular exercise or cleaning your teeth. You will never regret it.

Journey planning can vary from the simple provision of a street guide or map, which enables the salesman to plot his calls geographically, avoiding unnecessary travel or doubling back over the same territory, or a time chart which allocates a specific amount of time for each call.

At the end of each day – or selling period – the salesman should analyse how much of his precious time is spent actually 'face to face' with a customer and how much is spent in non-productive journeying. By critical analysis the salesman should be able to improve his 'selling time' and minimize his

'non-selling time'. Of course, travelling and planning and
pausing for lunch or a quick cup of tea are essential if the
salesman is not to become stale.

Sometimes it helps to create a points system for time spent
in various ways during the working day, like this, for
example:

Actual selling time (face to face with customer)	10 points
Actual selling time (on telephone with customer)	8 points
Planning calls (at home or office)	6 points
Travelling to and between calls	4 points
Non-business lunches, shoptalk with other reps	2 points

Why two points for the last item? Well, to be fair, a chat with
another salesman *can*, in certain circumstances, be like
hooking into an intelligence network and I therefore give
'shoptalk' the benefit of the doubt.

Clearly the serious salesman must aim to maximize points
on a daily basis by planning his journey time so that he can
spend most of it actually in the act of selling.

Keeping records is, I suspect, something of a chore to a lot
of salesmen. The phrase smacks of 'clerkish', bureaucratic
procedures, but it is an essential discipline particularly if the
salesman works direct from home without the back-up of a
secretary or office organization. With the recent explosion of
home computers, I believe the 'lone' salesman's future
working life will become dramatically transformed.

Stunning new information technology systems will enable
the most intricate and complex data to be stored about
customers' anticipated needs, past purchasing patterns, early
closing days and so forth, releasing precious time to be
exploited for the actual selling job.

Until you *are* computerized, however, you should aim to
build up a relevant database about your own particular
clients. Apart from the obvious information on average size
of order, reordering cycle and penetration of competitors'
products, you should create a special 'key' or code which will

jog your memory about any unusual characteristics associated with each client or his business.

A highly successful salesman I know, who makes a substantial living from marketing financial products such as savings plans, insurance-linked units and tax-effective bonds, *always* keeps special notes on all his major customers. He builds a complex dossier for them which acts as an excellent sales 'spur'.

At first glance my friend's dossier appears to be a catalogue of trivia, but he swears by it. It contains details of the client's wife's name and birthday, children's ages and birthdays, preferred holiday resorts and restaurants, choice of car, lists of hobbies and interests (stamp collecting, scuba diving, wrestling nude in vats of marmalade . . .), special features associated with client's house (pool, paddock, piano, tennis court, pet pigeons in loft, darkroom). No scrap of information – my friend tells me – is too insignificant to be excluded.

Now, the dossier is not compiled to fulfil some sinister, intrusive purpose, it is simply an *aide-mémoire* which keeps a two-way contact *even during those periods when the client is out of the buying cycle*. He will send a jokey, lighthearted card as birthdays come round. He will phone just prior to the annual holiday to wish bon voyage. He will clip newspaper or magazine reports which cover the client's hobbies with a 'Dear Jack, Thought you might have missed this' note.

When most other salesmen of financial products are at home watching television at the end of what they think has been a hard day, my friend is scrutinizing his card index system so that *tomorrow* another batch of his clients will receive that personal message or thoughtful gift that keeps *him* at the front of their minds until the next time he is face to face with them on a serious sales call.

Yes, it's hard work and means fitting the follow-up routine into an already tightly packed schedule.

My friend plans to retire at the age of forty-five with over half a million pounds in fat commissions salted away in his bank account. Riches and success don't drop out of the trees. They *have* to be worked for. So,

- Plan your journeys
- Maximize your real selling time
- Telephone if you can't visit
- Study your work pattern and eliminate wasteful travelling
- Keep good records
- Stay 'front of mind' with your clients by creative thinking
- If you're a lone wolf salesman, save up fast for a home computer
- If you're *office* based, make sure *their* records are what *you* want in order to sell
- *Anticipate* anniversaries, whether they mark the client's wedding, his becoming a grandfather, getting promoted or signing his first contract with you

Remember, opportunity knocks many times in a salesman's life but the dumb salesman is hardly ever listening. If you *organize* your life and work *constructively*, you can make your own luck. The biggest breaks come not to the workshy poseur in the pub but to the man or woman who believes that *persistence* overcomes all known obstacles.

9. Techniques of Persuasion

Changing other people's opinions

Avoiding arguments in favour of bold assertions

Attempting to cause a 'change of mind' in others is not exclusive to the professional salesman. Teachers, politicians, actors and scientists all do it to a greater or lesser degree, sometimes unconsciously.

Trying to change the opinions of one's fellows is an activity which predates recorded history and even literacy – it is linked, perhaps, with the development of speech itself. The line that divides 'changing people's opinions by persuasion' and 'one-sided propaganda' is gossamer thin. Not all propaganda is bad of course. Governments use it to try and stop us smoking, or driving too fast, or to persuade us that certain types of food are harmful. In its purest form propaganda is deliberately manipulative and one-sided. It exists *not* to encourage debate or doubt, but to *change people's minds*. It is concerned with achieving a predetermined response from those to whom it is directed.

In less salubrious societies than our own, governments utilize fear, or threats of direct violence, to force acceptance of the propaganda being communicated. Even in Britain the anti-smoking lobby prefers to dwell on the negative areas, listing smoking-related diseases as a reason for 'changing your mind', and rarely extols the *benefits* of non-smoking.

In the commercial world the salesman must accept that a large part of his role will be to 'change people's minds'. In this sense, he or she will have to flirt with the same techniques of persuasion that are employed by the propagandist.

The salesman must not be squeamish about this fact.

Academics may exist to encourage debate, inspire questioning, challenge accepted forms, and so on. The salesman is not in the business of encouraging debate for its own sake. The harsh reality is that the salesman will only encourage debate as a means to securing his goal – which is to change people's minds, or, to put it more succinctly, to make people accept his arguments as being, if not infallible, then certainly as holding a monopoly of 'truth'. Thus the techniques of persuasion must be learned by the aspiring commercial salesman and we will examine them in this chapter.

Rational and dispassionate argument so beloved by Socrates is a totally different discipline which causes more questions to be raised than answers to be supplied. Selling is about providing answers. It therefore follows that the salesman must *already* know both the questions *and* the answers if he wishes to predetermine any meeting.

Does this mean that the salesman must be partial and suppress information, feeding his subject only with facts which reinforce and hasten the approach of his objective? The answer is yes. The successful salesman *must* be partial and if suppressing information is too rich for your blood – how about 'the selective choice of facts' as an alternative?

Shopkeepers put their best goods in the window – so must salesmen. It is the partial and selective view of a particular subject, item or service that the salesman offers to his prospects.

Talk of totally 'unbiased' presentations by sellers to buyers with 'all the facts, warts and all' on the negotiating table is a load of sanctimonious old cobblers. Everybody is selective in an argument. Everybody marshals his chosen facts to provide the greatest strength for the case he is making. Like lawyers who have to defend clients in court. They have to dig and ferret for snippets of information that will shed the most favourable light on their man in the dock.

At least salesmen have a real choice. If you don't feel you can act as a propagandist for your product (in the true sense of the word – i.e., from the Latin *propagare*, which means, in horticultural parlance, the practice of grafting fresh shoots of a plant into the soil to grow into a life of their own!), then either don't become a salesman or pick a product or service you do feel hot about.

Remember, the propagandist (salesman) rarely, if ever, argues, but makes strong assertions about the concept he is discussing. The essence of successful propaganda is the selective presentation of attractive facts. This is not the same as lying. The distinction is, or should be, crystal clear.

A woman, otherwise plain, who is complimented on the lustrous nature of her hair, will instinctively promote and project that desirable feature. Likewise a man, undistinguished but for his resonant voice, will make much of this lucky gift. Deliberately exposing your bad points, whether personal or corporate, defies logical explanation outside of a psychiatrist's consulting room, and salesmen should have no hang-ups about aggressively selecting what is best about the product or service they are selling.

In the modern world, where sophisticated advertising brings the hustle of the bazaar right into your living-room via the television screen, a particular problem exists.

It is the problem of *competitive excellence*. Simply stated, this means that the standardization of production and packaging creates a range of products that are almost indistinguishable from one another. Soap, soup, chocolate, mass-produced clothing, freezers, cookers, cleaning fluids, airlines, building societies, banks, etc. In most of these fields the first three or four brand leaders are all of a *uniformly high standard*. They are technically advanced and scrupulously researched. How, then, does the consumer make the choice? And, more importantly, why does the consumer make a choice at all? Why doesn't he buy at random? Why does brand loyalty exist?

The fulcrum is the 'added' or 'perceived' value of a product. Advertising people prefer to describe it as investing the product with 'personality' – making it 'sexy', more 'appealing'.

A soap powder sexy? Who are we kidding? No, it's a serious point. Megamillions are spent each year just injecting 'personality' differences into products which are virtually identical.

The lesson to be drawn from this for all aspiring salesmen is pretty straightforward. However similar your product or service is to the competition, it's up to *you* to invest it with charisma, uniqueness, special qualities.

OK, let's pause here to consider the practicality of such a technique. Can it work on sophisticated buyers? Yes, and it *does*. All the time. Non-stop. Why do you fall in love with a particular human being? They've all got legs, arms, teeth, hair, lips. Aren't they all identical?

To a Martian, yes. To *us*, not a chance. But it's a hell of a jump from the myriad nuances of the human personality to the 'perceived' differences between two brands of milk chocolate.

Or is it? Ever tried blind-tasting your favourite chocolate bar against the one you *never* buy? Could you tell the difference? What motivates you to choose the one at the expense of the other is an invisible ingredient injected into the product called 'personality'.

Salesmanship is about *individualizing your product or service* to make it more *desirable* than anything else.

So, in addition to knowing the *tangible* benefits that might exist in your product or service, i.e., price advantage, proven technical or performance superiority, attractive style, longer durability, etc., give it that extra 'fizz', that magical, elusive, intangible thing called 'personality'.

In many cases your company's advertising agents will have done the job for you, but there are still plenty of salesmen out there in the commercial jungle *without* the benefit of mass advertising support. To these pioneers, more than most, the creation of a *favourable product image* is utterly essential.

Remember, what you are selling is *never* just a physical item or a stated service. To jump ahead of the competition or stay out in front of the herd, you've got to breathe *life* into that proposition. Make that can of beans or that bloody heat pump as desirable as a raft to a drowning man.

It's back to that old, *primeval* sales commandment.

**Thou shalt create a burning need for thy product –
and then satisfy it.**

10. Success-sharing and Face-saving
The human factor

I don't wish to imply that in every salesman's briefcase there lurks a psychiatrist's couch, but I *do* believe that a mild interest in, and a slight knowledge of, the human psyche can be invaluable as a sales aid.

Success-sharing? What does it mean? Is it just another mantra to be chanted alongside phrases like 'meaningful dialogue' or 'in-depth analyses'?

What success-sharing means is working *constantly* towards closing the sale *in such a way that leaves the buyer feeling as triumphant as the seller*. This admirable state of affairs is not purely altruistic. A satisfied client is more likely to *remain* a client and most salesmen need *repeat purchase patterns* to be established early in a commercial relationship.

The first steps in achieving this are based upon the old-fashioned virtues of courtesy and common sense. It *pays* to open your negotiations *aware* of your client's perceptions about you, your company and its products. If a warm, trusting link has already been forged, you must build on it – and treat it as a precious item that can *easily be damaged*.

If, for example, you have established a considerable track record in after-sales service, be certain your *own* company knows how vital it is to *this* particular customer. Your call reports should emphasize how *impressed* the client is with the service – make a point of thanking your service department. To keep the positive perceptions healthy, you must *constantly* review and nurture them.

If, on the other hand, your negotiations open with a

frustrated or angry client, *you must be prepared to allow him time to let off steam*.

Let us take as a hypothetical example our ubiquitous heat pump salesman. He walks into the buyer's office to be greeted with an angry, disappointed client. Far from securing an immediate repeat offer for the Super XL5, he has to endure listening to a catalogue of complaints about its recent performance.

Golden Rule Number One. *Let the client have his say without interruption*.

Why? Well, most people *need* the therapy of venting their frustration on somebody else. Their anger will diminish and purge *itself* the longer you allow them to 'sound off'.

Golden Rule Number Two. *Do not be too quick or glib with your response to a complaint*.

It may sound trivial – even trumped up – but to the client *at that moment* it is probably *critical to his self-esteem* that you do not minimize his displeasure. Let him minimize it himself. And he will. After the torrent of words, he is likely to pause and say something like, 'Look I'm sorry to blow my top, but it's been one hell of a morning.'

Or, 'I don't want to sound *too* heavy, you understand – but it's *my* neck on the block. Old Rutherford, the financial director, has given me a bit of a roasting.'

Or, 'Please don't take this personally . . .'

Or, best of all, 'I'm sorry I lost my temper.'

All the above responses, or phrases very similar to them, will come spontaneously from the complainant if you let his opening outburst run its natural course.

Even if you have an *instant*, easily applied solution to the problem – don't *trump* him with it. He must be allowed to wallow – just a little – in the luxury of his own indignation. When you offer the solution, offer it sympathetically; acknowledge the client's frustration, tell him you *appreciate* how badly he feels. Any overdefensive reaction on your part will lead either to an argument or a *loss of face* for the client.

Now, loss of face is not quite so delicate an issue in the

Western world as it is, say, in Japan, but it is nevertheless an important consideration.

Let us assume that the client's complaints are unfounded. The Super XL5 didn't fail because of a mechanical fault, but because a connecting cable was severed by one of his *own* workmen. (OK – this is only an imaginary example!)

Accompanied by the still-bristling customer, you visit the site on his premises where the Super XL5 is installed and presto! You discover the broken cable. What you *don't* do, of course, is swing round on the client and say, 'It's the *cable*, you bombastic shit!'

Or, 'I *knew* it wasn't the pump . . .'

Or even, 'Well, *that* was a bit of a non-event.'

This is the moment – and it is *absolutely critical* – when you must bottle up your annoyance and find a way to save *the client's face*. Individual circumstances will determine just *what* form of words you use but they *must* be placatory, *understanding* and sympathetic.

He will know he's made a total asshole of himself – he doesn't need you to remind him. His response – if you don't take advantage of his discomfiture – will be one of relief and gratitude and you will have laid an important foundation stone in building your future relationship.

OK. What if the bloody XL5 turns out to be a piece of crap? Your assembly staff have dropped a teaspoon in the works, and the fisheye socket wheel brace has sheared off making the whole contraption give off blue smoke and a noise like a whale fornicating in a tin shed. When this happens, you must learn to *share* your client's frustration. Get inside his skin. Express your annoyance and, once again, indicate how you understand his disappointment at *your* equipment's failure.

And then get it put right as quickly as you can. Even if it means *pressurizing* your own service staff. Once the fault is corrected, treat that client like you would a convalescent after a short illness. Try to fit in an extra call each month until you are satisfied that your relationship is back on an even keel.

The virtues of diplomacy are hard to categorize but they

are important tools in the hands of a conscientious salesman. By allowing the client to do all the 'head-butting', you are leaving yourself free to act as the knight in shining armour who retrieves a situation which would otherwise become ugly. And it becomes ugly when the salesman overreacts or tries to retaliate in a 'point-scoring way' to a client's outburst. Once *that* happens, both sides are dug into entrenched positions and will find it difficult to avoid becoming, even unconsciously, *adversaries*.

Perhaps the best way to approach the 'angry client' syndrome is to assume the role of a non-medical doctor. When a patient is ill, or in pain, or frightened – *no matter how bad he feels* – the doctor remains cool, concerned and professional.

So must you. Save your flights of passion, rhetoric and ebullience for the *positive* part of the meeting when you are once again extolling the virtues and benefits *to the customer* of what you are selling.

Similar principles apply if, in the absence of any specific complaint, you detect that the client is in a 'hard' mood. By 'hard' I mean intractable. Faintly belligerent. He catalogues, with much finger-wagging, what he is *not* prepared to accept.

This negative bargaining posture is unfortunately quite common, and it is of supreme importance for the salesman to *gently* move the client away from what he *doesn't* want or *won't* accept, to the much more fruitful area of what he *wants* and what he is *willing* to accept.

Don't fall into the trap of responding to a *negative bargaining* ploy with a negative of your own. Meetings at which buyer and seller only swap details of what they *won't* do, *can't* do or *mustn't* do will never blossom into sensible, creative negotiations where *success is shared* and *faces are saved*.

Freud may have been a long-winded, whiskery old foreigner, but he knew a few things about what made people tick. So should you.

Study people. Read Desmond Morris's *Manwatching*

(published by Jonathan Cape) and try to build up a mental dossier about the character-signposts of your own clients. There's an old Irish saying which goes, 'People are the same the world over 'cept for one damn thing – they're *all different.*'

Finally, here's a summary of dos and don'ts when facing a difficult client.

Don't argue	*Do* listen
Don't apply pressure	*Do* negotiate
Don't dig in	*Do* leave room to manoeuvre
Don't make counter-threats	*Do* offer solutions
Don't demand one-sided benefits in return for helping to solve the problem	*Do* emphasize the benefits that will accrue to *him* when the problem is solved
Don't make excuses which damage *your* company	*Do* acknowledge you may not be perfect
Don't be too glib with your solutions	*Do* merchandise them so that the client perceives them as 'benefits'
Don't gloat if the complaint is groundless	*Do* help him *save face*
Don't hog the limelight when you've solved the problem	*Do* let him *share* your *success*

11. Who Loves Ya, Baby?

Must you be liked to be successful?
The elimination of guilt and other
negative vibrations

Not everybody likes a salesman. Indeed, most recent surveys rank salesmen about as unpopular as politicians and tax inspectors (but not *quite* as unpopular as traffic wardens and VAT men). So, take heart. There's always somebody worse off than you.

Way back in the 1950s, the distinguished economist J. K. Galbraith set down in his book, *The Affluent Society* (published by Houghton Mifflen), some of his thoughts about salesmanship. He still holds a somewhat jaundiced view of free enterprise and the tainted fruit it produces in abundance. *Most* products, he argues, aren't necessary at all. They fill no *real* need, merely an *imaginary* need. Since demand for these products couldn't exist were it not *contrived*, then the whole manufacturing, advertising and selling cycle is synthetic.

The function of the salesman, therefore, is to *create desire* – to bring into being *wants* that previously did not exist. Advertising men have been known to describe this process as '*modern want-creation*'.

Galbraith and other undeniably brilliant academics condemn it as a trivial, almost demeaning human activity. So entrenched is this antipathy towards salesmanship that sales organizations themselves have become apologetic, even neurotic, about prosecuting their legitimate and vital interests. We have all seen the coupon advertisement in the Sunday papers which announces, with megaphone defensiveness, 'No salesman will call!'

Of course, certain types of salesman can give offence and

I am no different from the average consumer in abhorring the foot-in-the-door, glib, insincere huckster who tries to con you into buying something by chicanery. Or by pretending he is conducting a 'survey'. If anybody knocks on your door and announces that he is 'doing a survey on educational needs' in the area, the chances are he is trying to sell you an encyclopaedia or some other 'improving' device.

I have no qualms about being a salesman. Neither should the encyclopaedia rep. Let him stand up and be counted. Unless he is ashamed. In which case, he should quit and try something like market gardening. This said, let us return to the subject of 'creating need' which, after all, is an integral part of the selling ethos.

The academics scoff at the consumer society, secure in their ivory towers on the campus or in the panelled studies of the old universities. They sneer at ordinary people because their dreams are cheap. But their criticisms levelled at 'salesmanship' and 'non-essential consumership' are dubious in the extreme. Who is to decide what man's true needs are beyond food, shelter and sex? Do we really *need* fast cars, silk shirts, instant coffee, video recorders, sun-tan lotion, home computers, cufflinks, cosmetics, jewellery, wall-to-wall carpets? Of course we don't. But imagine how dull life would be if man's 'inherent desire for advancement' was confined only to basic needs.

It is the aspiring, acquisitive nature of man, along with his miraculous power of speech, that sets him apart from the beasts. At first, a cave and an animal skin was enough for his needs. As was a hunk of raw meat or a handful of nuts. Today, basic requirements in the industrialized world are much more sophisticated. The modern family, living in a council house with a bathroom, hot and cold running water, television, an electric cooker, maybe a washing machine and a small car, have a structure around them which so dramatically exceeds their *primary wants* as would make sixteenth-century man – were he briefly reincarnated – gasp with incredulity. Even to a nobleman in Henry VIII's court, the modern man with his kitchen, inside lavatory, warmth and comfort would be living a life of unimaginable luxury.

The definition of poverty has had to be refined in modern society. It is now a *relative* condition, *absolute* deprivation having long since been eliminated, at least in the West. Therefore, the perception of people's 'needs' in a dynamic, rapidly accelerating environment is inevitably blurred and mixed up with their *aspirations*.

The salesman should have no doubts about his role in this shifting kaleidoscope – he is there to *create*, *identify*, *magnify*, and ultimately *satisfy* a whole range of peripheral 'wants' and 'desires' as well as to create, identify and satisfy a raft of much more 'deserving' or 'serious' needs.

In a free society, a cornucopia of choice is one of the major benefits. That such a range of options includes the trivial, the useless and the downright shoddy is not, in itself, reason enough to denounce the system as wholly bad. Freedom includes the freedom to make mistakes, and to exercise personal taste, however gross it may seem to a professor of sociology at Harvard University. The pressure of competition acts as a natural selector. The salesman of bad products *cannot* survive for very long, however skilled he might be in the art of persuasion. Neither can he succeed if, in the words of famous advertising man Rosser Reeves, 'the product or service does not meet some desire or need of the consumer'.

It matters not a jot that the desire is 'created' by the salesman. Or the engineer who invents some new gadget for peeling grapes. Or the advertising agent who tricks it out in pretty colours. Or the neighbour who proudly exhibits his new purchase. As a salesman, you must learn to forget all the pussyfooting, half-baked sociological crap that academic theorists put about to justify their own existence.

The progress of man from the primeval swamps to the sophisticated technocratic society in which he finds himself is a story of uneven, occasionally chaotic growth. The real spur to progress has been – and always will be – a desire for self-improvement. And self-improvement has little or nothing to do with the simple satisfaction of *basic wants*.

So, rejoice that, as a salesman, you are part of the great wheel of progress. Celebrate your role as the implanter of new 'desires'. Be cheerful that by your persuasion and enthusiasm you can contribute something to keeping that great wheel turning.

Why are salesmen relatively unpopular? Why is their image sometimes tarnished by accusations of trickery, quackery and bamboozlement?

Well, first of all, let it be said *such charlatans do exist*. Far too many of them. But so do *bad* doctors and *dishonest* clergymen and *crooked* lawyers. They don't *all* get tarred with the same brush – why do salesmen? Perhaps it's in the nature of their trade. They exist to *make things happen*, to *force change*, to *persuade*, to *implant desires*.

These activities are uncomfortable to many, particularly Anglo-Saxons. In the USA it sometimes seems that everybody is a salesman. Their whole society is geared to 'doing a deal', 'making a pitch' and 'clinching a sale'.

There is no easy solution for the professional salesman. Like a politician he will be regarded with slight reserve, even suspicion. But that is an overview, a generalization. What the individual salesman can and *must* do is build a reputation of integrity and trust directly with his own customers. Be as dazzling and as dynamic as you like, but remember the old adage, 'You've got to take the customers *with* you.' And you can only take them with you if:

1. You are enthusiastic.
2. Knowledgeable.
3. Honest.
and
4. They trust you.
and
5. You have identified or created a *real desire* for what you are selling.

And remember also that it's what the customer takes *out* of your sales pitch that is far more important than what you put in.

To be successful doesn't necessarily mean you have to be liked or vice versa. But life will be a hell of a lot easier if you *are* liked. It's good business sense. Who wants to buy from a louse when he can buy from a nice guy?

And, finally, even if you aren't liked *enough* to please you, ask yourself this. Am I *respected*? Best to be both, of course, but at the end of the day, *respect* has to be a much more desirable quality than mere likeableness. Often one breeds the other. The *respected* rep you learn to like. Or the *likeable* rep you learn to respect.

Don't let the academics, or those with a pristine vision of how society *ought* to be, blow you off course. You're a salesman in the *real* world. You've got a job to do – it's *important*. Tell yourself that every morning when you look at your image in the bathroom mirror.

And get out there and *sell*.

12. Dealing with Rejection

No is a horrid word and you'll hear it often

While getting to 'yes' is the objective of all sales activity, the inescapable fact of a salesman's life is that he will hear 'no' far more frequently. Coping with rejection is therefore important if the salesman is not to become discouraged, depressed or even suicidal.

My very first solo call as a salesman brought me face to face with a huge café owner on London's Commercial Road. I had rehearsed my pitch with the dedication of a Shakespearean actor, learning to change the inflexion of my voice when I mentioned such devastating temptations as 'marrowfat peas' and 'catering packs of jellied oxtail soup'. With growing confidence I approached the climax of my introduction, watching the café owner's obvious fascination with my style.

At last I had finished, aglow with pride and surging adrenaline. The café owner, clad in a fetching string vest with grease-spot accessories, remained silent for a long moment. Then he shifted his huge bulk from one foot to the other and delicately picked his nose.

'Fuck off,' he explained.

The effect on me, as you can well imagine, was a trifle shattering. I had expected sales resistance – we'd been *trained* to deal with it after all. We had prepared for *all* eventualities hadn't we? We knew how to respond if he claimed his stock levels from last month's orders were still too high. We were ready with additional bulk discounts if the competition had tried to muscle in on our territory. We could throw in counter displays of tomato sauce bottles three-foot high, and wonderful cardboard calendars which featured seven ways to serve spaghetti in cheese sauce to the hungry lorry drivers who frequented such establishments.

What we didn't have answers for were requests to vanish in such quaint and forthright language. Frankly, I was devastated. There I was, twenty years old, stiff white collar and smart overcoat, new vinyl briefcase and bowler hat. (Yes, a bowler hat. Ye gods, I must have looked a *total* wally!)

I turned and fled the premises without uttering another single word. This was my *first* call ever and I had registered total, unmitigated failure. I was a disaster. And I was still supposed to make ten more calls that day.

I took myself into a Lyons Corner House and over a cup of tea I decided that I couldn't face another sales call *ever*. I had made a gross error in choosing such a career – it was all too awful to contemplate. After the cup of tea I would find a telephone box, ring head office and tell *them* what the café owner had just told me.

I actually got as far as dialling the office number and at the moment of connection I caught a glimpse of myself in the little mirror that phone boxes have on the wall. I looked pathetic. A bowler-hatted twit with an expression of sanctimonious self-pity on his face. I had heard swearwords before. Army life had seen to that. It wasn't the *language*, it was the *rejection* that had completely punctured my self-confidence.

I didn't complete the phone call. I gathered up my vinyl briefcase and decided to have *one* more stab at it. I wish I could say that the second call was a roaring success. It wasn't. But the rejection was less scourging and at least I had the opportunity to discuss business for the *next* month. By lunchtime I was getting into my stride and had actually written out a couple of big, fat orders.

I don't know to this day what precisely triggered me into staying with it – for a while in that Lyons Corner House I was ready to quit for ever. Whatever it was, I'm grateful for it.

Later, much later, I learnt that the café owner who had so vigorously rejected my overtures was often used as a launching pad for new salesmen. The theory, unofficial though it was, seemed to be that if you could survive *that* you'd survive anything.

To put rejection in perspective is never easy. Particularly when it's *you* who's being rejected. An old friend of mine, Melville Mark, who for years ran a public relations consultancy in Geneva, used to remind me of the 'need to persist' by telling me a little fable.

A young man – he would explain – once stood on the corner of New Bond Street and Piccadilly politely asking ladies if they would like to favour him with a kiss. He got his face slapped twenty-three times before lunch.

But he also got kissed twice. Which was a one hundred per cent success rate compared to the man who wouldn't even stand on the corner!

So, however you trick it out, if you're a salesman you're going to have to live with a certain amount of negative vibes from time to time. But they can be minimized. Rejection doesn't have to be courted.

If I had known what I know now on that first fateful call in Commercial Road, I would have played it differently. Maybe treated the call as simply an introduction, avoiding the straight sales pitch until I had got the measure of the man.

If you sense a massive 'no' coming on in the middle of your meeting, *you must immediately find something* the client will say 'yes' to. Spotting the impending negative is a matter of instinct as well as judgement.

An insurance salesman I know will neutralize any approaching 'no' by offering a strings-free analysis of the client's current financial package. He will go so far as to actually say, 'Forgive me, sir, I don't think it would be right for you to make a buying decision at this moment – and I wouldn't wish to press you. I'd very much like to make a more detailed appraisal of your existing savings plans – *entirely* without obligation and then perhaps we can have a further meeting.'

This technique usually prevents the 'no' hitting you between the eyes like a sockful of wet sand. It also gives you time to get your act together for next time when the client may be in a more receptive frame of mind.

And if there *is* a next time, give the client something to say 'yes' to early on in the call.

Selling effectively is a *gentle art*, and the technique of side-stepping the negatives can only be truly effective if you develop a lightness of touch. With few exceptions, people prefer harmony to conflict, agreement to dispute and, of course, much prefer saying 'yes' than 'no'. They will say 'yes' more frequently and more willingly if you ease them into the habit by your skills as a *talker*, *explainer*, *counsellor* and *benefit-provider*.

When all is said and done, however, if you're determined to be a salesman there will still be a plethora of 'nos'. I'm sorry, but that's life. You didn't *really* think selling was going to be all plain sailing, did you? If you can't stand the heat, don't sit on the stove in your underpants.

Does getting a 'no' lobbed at my head still worry me?

Why should I lie to you? Yes. I *hate* it. Even now. But I've learned to be philosophical about it, to ride it like a punch and stay in there still pitching.

Unless of course you've been foolish enough to try and sell a really *tacky* product or service. If you're into *bad* merchandise no amount of effort or psyching up will ever overcome the barrage of negatives with which your presentation will be greeted. You'll be like the photographic rep in Golders Green trying to flog pictures of Hitler's barmitzvah to the local newspaper. And you'd hate that, wouldn't you?

So don't let 'no' knock the stuffing out of *you*. One good 'yes' from time to time will more than compensate, believe me.

13. Closing the Sale

The climax of all sales effort is that moment when the client says, 'Yes, I'll buy.' Closing the sale, therefore, must be a clearly defined goal for which the salesman has prepared himself and one which he is confidently anticipating. Too many salesmen go into a meeting actually expecting failure. When I was a food rep in the 1950s, I heard a salesman saying, 'I'm scheduled to call on so-and-so today. He's a hopeless case – he never buys – but I need his name on my call report.' Obviously such a negative mental attitude will make closing the sale a preordained disaster.

Each and every call must have the seeds of success within it – and the first step is inside the salesman's head. He's got to *believe* he's going to clinch the order; without that belief he might as well be at home stripping wallpaper or repairing his wife's vibrator.

I like to avoid rigid patterns or strict formulas, but there is, however, a broad sequence of events that should be followed if a sale is to be closed quickly and efficiently. The first set of principles apply to *preparation*, and the second set to *execution*. Let's go through them carefully.

Preparation

1. Is my product knowledge up to date?
2. Have I made an appointment with the *real* decision-maker?
3. Am I briefed on the client's business, his supply situation, his past buying patterns, his prejudices, his enthusiasms?

4. Am I going to need a full *sales pitch* to inform the client of my product's advantages or just a *succinct reprise*? (Remember, many a sale has been lost by boring the ass off a prospect who's heard your story before.)

5. How much time is the client likely to put at my disposal? (Avoid seeing *anybody* who says, 'I've only got five minutes.' He's never going to sit still long enough for you to sink your hooks in.)

6. Rehearse your opening. *Yes*, rehearse it. Get quickly to the point. Avoid too much social banter. Don't start the pitch with a joke – ever!

7. Be *early* for the appointment. Five minutes is plenty. Good salesmen are *never*, *ever* late.

Execution

1. If it's a first meeting, introduce yourself and your company clearly and crisply.

2. Thank the client for putting his time at your disposal.

3. Open with a reference to *his* business, *not* yours. Remember, the *only thing* that is of the slightest importance to him is how your product or service can improve *his* business. (He doesn't give a monkey's fart about the fact that your company was incorporated in 1898 – or that you've just moved to new premises in Theydon Bois.)

4. As you describe your product benefits, and you should major on *no more* than three at a time, relate them directly to the prospect's own company.

   'Mr Drake, our heat pumps produce 10 per cent more energy than the competition, which should prove valuable in your own factory. In the last company report your chairman indicated that rising fuel costs were a constant pressure on profits. We believe that by installing our product, which is no more expensive than any others on the market, you can make a significant contribution to your company's profitability. Let me briefly explain how . . .'

5. Try and introduce a compelling reason why he should say 'yes' *now*, i.e., fast delivery, impending price or VAT increases.
6. Quantify the benefits he will obtain by buying your product.
7. Leave price till last, unless he's a regular customer and you're negotiating repeat business.
8. Have the contract or agreement ready. All he needs to do is sign.
9. Take command of the situation, even if he puts up sales resistance.
10. Never *directly* disagree with any statement he makes.

   'Of course you're right, Mr Drake, our Super XL5 heat pump is not cheap, but it will provide you with *exactly* the performance you need – the smaller version will be more expensive in the long run.'
11. Maintain eye contact. This will keep his attention.
12. Treat all objections as questions to be answered. Answer them fully and push on.
13. When he has said 'yes', and signed, keep your post-coital social chat to a minimum. Many a sale has been won – and then lost, by the salesman hanging around and dropping his guard.

An acquaintance of mine clinched a corporate insurance deal for over £100,000. The prospect had shaken hands and was just waiting for a second signature on the document from his partner in the firm – a mere formality. The partner, who was in the next office, was on a transatlantic telephone call and my acquaintance began to pass the time in idle chat. Within minutes he revealed his political prejudices about the Middle East, referring to a particular nation in unflattering terms.

The client's face froze and he became obviously uncomfortable. Still the salesman chuntered on, glowing with fatuous satisfaction at a job well done, until the door opened and the partner came into the room. He was from the same country that the salesman had been slagging off. Result? No sale. And a prospect killed stone dead for all time.

So, remember, when you've won – get the hell *out*, but gracefully. Or, as a forthright American millionaire said to one of his food salesmen who was introducing a new line of fruit pies to the buyer for a huge restaurant chain in California, 'When the order is secure, don't hang about like a piece of spare furniture, leave – even if just to celebrate by taking a flying fuck at a rolling doughnut.'

The most successful salesmen are those who can orchestrate a meeting so that the client truly and permanently believes that he *bought* and you didn't actually *sell*.

If you are empowered to offer prices below list or unscheduled discounts, *never open with these inducements*. Price-cutting is a delicate instrument. If a prospect senses desperation, i.e., an instant 'offer', he will become suspicious. Always kick off with product *benefits*, *user-advantages*, *profit-enhancement*.

If the game is moving your way you may not need to discount. Use it as a last resort. If your product or service is good – and what the hell are you doing selling it if it isn't? – then stick to your price. You must put a value on what you offer, and the value you place on it is significant in helping the client judge what you and your company are all about. And there must be a good wholesome reason for offering a discount. By that I mean a *tangible* benefit to *both* sides of the deal.

'Mr Drake, I understand you have 34 separate packing sheds on the plant. If you take a minimum of 20 of our Super XL5 heat pumps we can offer you a volume discount of 5 per cent.'

What if the client then says, 'I only want 17 – can I have the same discount?'

How you deal with this proposition depends on two things:

1. Is 5 per cent for 20 the fixed company policy?
2. Is your offer the first tier in a structured negotiating ploy?

Be careful. A clever buyer will get you very close to thinking the sale is clinched and then take the initiative by pressing for massive price cuts. If your first offer – 5 per cent in this imaginary case – is your best, say so.

'Mr Drake, like you, we price our goods very carefully. An order of below 20 at 5 per cent discount would give my company less than an acceptable profit.'

Don't undervalue your merchandise. This, however, is the moment for you to take the initiative again.

'Mr Drake, why not take one of our Super XL5 pumps for each of your 34 packing sheds? If you can go to that [pause] I can offer you a saving on the whole deal of 10 per cent.'

All I am trying to illustrate here is the importance of maintaining the initiative. *You* must call the shots while at the same time providing the client with *powerful* reasons why he should buy from you.

Remember, he may have second thoughts *after* you've left. Try to anticipate them and give him *all* the plus answers he needs when thinking about the deal or discussing it with his superiors – if he has any.

Listen to your customer. You can still dominate a meeting even when he's doing the talking. If he wanders from the subject, *politely* interrupt and ask him a question that will force him to return to the straight and narrow.

Dale Carnegie knew the value of asking *relevant* questions. He always gave the client an opportunity to display his knowledge and he rarely missed the chance to allow his client to talk at length about his chosen subject.

A couple of blindingly obvious points are:

Never knock *your* company . . . or your boss.

Never knock your competitors. How do you know your client hasn't bought from them in the past? Attack them and you may be casting doubts on his judgement. Better by far to praise the competition and then move on to describe why your company is *even better*.

Learn to recognize when you've drawn an irrevocably short straw. If the client says, 'Well, it's not my decision actually, it's Mr Thrustbuttock's really, and he's on holiday,' or 'I'm leaving next month and my successor doesn't start till Tuesday,' or even 'My son works for the competition,' get up and leave – with suitable excuses.

If the client is drunk, don't stay, even for a chat. Don't accept abuse, either, about your company or yourself. We all come across the occasional pig from time to time and we should cut our losses and move on – quickly. Never argue, because you lose even if you win. It's better to quit. Don't invest in failure. Only painful experience will teach you how to recognize the truly useless asshole of a client – and when you do, leave him to the competition.

Finally, make damn sure you or your company can *deliver* what you *promise*. Nothing makes people more angry than a salesman who bamboozles an order out of a client by spurious product claims or hyped-up benefits. Let the only surprise your client gets when he finally receives your product or service be a pleasant one. And, after a decent interval, call him and ask him how his company is benefiting from his decision to buy from you.

People will buy, and go on buying from you, so long as *they* and their companies *see*, *feel*, *experience* and *enjoy* tangible benefits from making that choice. The salesman who finds out what a client *really wants* and then *supplies* it will soon become a star.

14. The Telephone
Salesman's friend? Or foe?

The phone call as an ice-breaker and other guidelines

We all use the telephone. Every day. It is now an integral part of the fabric of our business and social lives. In America, a man actually died when his phone was cut off and the verdict was 'Death from heart seizure induced by an excess of anguish brought on by isolation from the instrument he treated as a lifeline to the world.'

To the salesman, a telephone can be his single most important piece of sales equipment. But misused it can kill a sale faster than halitosis in a love affair.

There are obvious basic common-sense rules about how to use the telephone which every salesman should scrupulously observe. Here are a few of them (we'll get to 'content' and 'technique' later).

When making a phone call

Speak clearly

Don't press the instrument too close to your mouth – that will distort your voice. About two inches from your lips is fine.

Always allow a beat of two seconds between your prospect saying 'Hello, Mr Brown' or 'Tadcot 63810' and you launching into your sales patter.

Why? The human ear takes about that long to adjust to the change of scale necessary to engage in a phone conversation, and the opening words in a phone call which is too hurried are often blurred or lost. It also puts you at a psychological disadvantage if you are asked to repeat something so early in the proceedings.

If you know you have a bad line, full of whistles and crackling, *you* suggest re-dialling before the client does. Never try and 'press on regardless' against a barrage of static or a crossed line.

Never *slam* the phone down. I know it looks dramatically conclusive on television and there will be occasions when the obduracy of Mr Lumpfuttock of Slough – the senior processed-sausage buyer – will make you wish you could ram the receiver down his throat. But the 'effect' of slamming down the phone is grossly overrated. You, the slammer-down, can hear that satisfying 'crash' and it may make *you* feel better. The chap at the other end, even old Lumpfuttock of Slough, God rot his entrails, only hears the customary click. Once your phone is down he can't hear the echoing waves of sound that fill your office after the event, or see your secretary's face drained of its customary healthy colour.

Speak 'naturally'. Do avoid putting on a 'special' telephone voice. Nothing is more transparent than the phoney accent on the telephone – the instrument has the uncanny ability of magnifying speech defects and long-forgotten traces of regional accents. So please shun talking about 'thysands of pines' or 'rows of terraced hizes'. Just be yourself. But slower. Most people tend to gallop during telephone conversations and for the sales call, this can be fatal.

Breathing. Yes, we all do it. But a lot of breathy exhalations down the little telephone tube can sound either like the start of an obscene phone call or a cry for help from a drowning idiot.

Sniffing, gulping, burping and tooth-sucking all get magnified on the telephone and they all sound absolutely *ghastly*. So get your belching and snorting over and done with *before* that important call.

Technique and content

Here are a few pointers on technique. They do not constitute the definitive list because the only way to become *really* expert on the telephone is to go on a real-life telephone sales course and actually use the instrument while learning. Nevertheless the following may help you improve your style.

Be authoritative. 'Is Mr McAlpine there?' is not strong enough. 'May I speak to Mr McAlpine please?' is much better. It has the timbre of command about it and will establish you, the caller, as a person of substance. Always pitch your voice *up* a little when you pronounce the name of the man or woman you are trying to speak with.

Once your call has been *initially successful*, i.e., you've got who *you* want on the other end of the line, *get to the point quickly*. Say who you are, even if a secretary has just switched you through to her boss, and state your company name. *Don't* waffle on about the weather or how difficult it has been to make the connection. Even if you're calling a well-known client. Small talk, with friends too, can take place *when the real purpose* of the call has been achieved.

Don't waste time on the 'Mr Ritzfleischer-is-not-here-right-now-but-I'm-his-second-in-command' type of person. If you have *predetermined* who the decision-maker is – the man who actually has the authority to say yes or sign the cheque or both – don't waste your pitch on a second-stringer. He'll pass on the message. Of course he will. But through a distorting filter that will drain out all *your* enthusiasm, commitment and logic.

If you sense you have drawn a really short straw and made contact with an asshole of Olympic proportions, don't wait for him to ring off – *you must do it first*. As the Americans say, 'You must establish yourself as the rejector not the rejectee.' But that never means 'cutting him dead'. That's about as sterile as phone slamming. If Ritzfleischer's second-in-command, a hopeless nitwit called Wimple, starts becoming evasive, you must be ready to *anticipate* the pattern of events, thus:

Wimple: I'm afraid Mr Ritzfleischer's not available right now. Can I help you?

You: Thanks, but I would prefer to speak with Mr Ritzfleischer personally.

Wimple: Look, I know that Mr Ritzfleischer is going to be very busy for the next few days – why don't you tell me what it is you want to talk about? I'll pass the message on to Mr Ritzfleischer.

You: Thanks very much. I appreciate your help but I'd prefer to try again when Mr Ritzfleischer *is* available. Goodbye.

You *know* Wimple is a wimp. You can tell, can't you? And it is better to press on with the next call than waste time throwing your best sales lines at the equivalent of a brick wall.

Not all phone calls *can* be selling calls of course. Certain propositions can only be made on a face-to-face basis and the phone is just a means of fixing the appointment. When fixing such meetings by phone, be *precise* about your business. No 'we're conducting a survey' crap. You have a 'benefit' to offer this client, haven't you? If he buys what you're selling, it's going to do *him* and his company some good, isn't it? Well, isn't it?

When fixing the appointment 'offer a benefit'.

You: I'd appreciate twenty minutes of Mr McAlpine's time next week to show him how our trucklesnudgers can increase your yield per acre by as much as 10 per cent.

or

          I have a proposal for Mr McAlpine, which I'd like to develop in detail, but in broad terms it could enable your company's products to reach more customers than they ever reached before.

If there is no 'benefit' in seeing a salesman, why see him in the first place? As a general rule, face-to-face selling is more effective than ear-to-ear selling on the telephone, but there are some exceptions.

Most national and regional newspapers have highly trained telesales teams who canvass for classified advertising *exclusively* on the telephone. Their techniques are polished, simple, direct and, above all, brief. They go from introduction, to proposition, to *close* very swiftly indeed. They have mastered the art of using a 'few words' effectively and that's the key to success.

If you don't fancy going on a telephone sales technique course right now, try tape-recording some of your own sales calls instead. You'll be surprised what a burbling idiot you sound while on the phone. But take heart. Practice *can* make you very much better.

15. Selling by Audiovisual Presentation
The twentieth-century nightmare

Selling is no longer a question of ramming your foot in the door and rattling off the old sales patter to a bewildered householder in an apron and curlers. Salesmanship has come of age, like seamless tights and disposable nappies, and not infrequently these days salesmen and saleswomen are required to deliver their precious pitch in front of an invited audience – from a stage or podium. If such a prospect drives you whimpering into the nearest pub, this chapter is not for you – or indeed for anybody else who is squeamish.

On those occasions when a salesperson is on display, before a sceptical throng, the qualities needed to acquit oneself honourably are many and varied. Nerves of steel can be useful, especially if coupled with bowels of concrete. And, above all, one must master the technique of *acting*. Yes, presenting to an audience – make *no* mistake about this – is a theatrical performance. Appearance, dress sense, hairstyle are all important. Preparation and rehearsal are the vital keys, and on the big day itself a certain tension, a soupçon of adrenaline howling through the veins, are ingredients without which no truly great presentation can be achieved. But is it really *selling*?

Has any audiovisual presentation ever persuaded even one member of the audience to whom it was directed to rush breathlessly from the conference chamber and actually purchase something that the speaker was promoting?

An unfair question! I hear you expostulate. Surely not all audiovisual presentations are selling vehicles. Aren't some of them exercises in the distribution of knowledge? Wrong. All audiovisual presentations in front of live audiences are conscious or unconscious acts of salesmanship or – if you prefer it in these groggy days of neurotic equality – acts of salespersonship.

I once visited the ancient city of Vienna where a clutch of clever people had conducted a seminar on, among other things, market research. Normally, forty-minute diatribes on econometrics, price elasticity and media imperative analyses are not immediately associated with the desire to sell or even persuade. On close inspection, however, I have reached the firm and unshakeable conclusion that all participants in the great circus of audiovisual presentations are as much involved in the trade of selling as the bloke in Berwick Street Market who flogs Hong Kong shirts at half-price to vulnerable punters during their lunch hour. For the researcher, steeped in theory, his qualifications gleaned from learned texts, the audiovisual presentation is a seductive opportunity to emerge from the cluttered anonymity of the backroom and sell to real people.

But the hazards are legion, and all ambitious salespeople should beware of them. You see, there is a thing called 'Murphy's Law of Presentations', and it goes something like this.

Whatever mechanical, audiovisual or constructional aids you have organized for your presentation will not only go wrong, but actually turn round and bite you in the throat.

For example, some years ago I was giving a little talk in Plymouth to a group of venerable West Country pharmacists, and illustrating my pearls of wisdom by means of a carousel projector. Now this is a fine piece of equipment, as everybody knows, and the operational technique is essentially simple. However, when I pressed the button for the first slide, Murphy struck and the machine jammed solid.

Being of a highly sensitive and mechanical disposition, I

gave it a quick thump. It fell off the table, wrenching its cable with it, and landed on the foot of a leading Cornish pharmacist who, believe it or believe it not, had only the previous week suffered an operation for in-growing toenails.

Moving with speed and precision, I switched on a TV monitor (which I had arranged to be cunningly linked to a VCR machine with standby material) and assured my audience that the presentation would continue at once.

It did, but not entirely the way I had intended. Mysteriously, my VCR tape had been switched by persons unknown and instead of a riveting illustration of how the sales of nasal decongestants in the West Country exceeded that of all the Benelux countries put together, my audience of pharmacists were treated to an 'out-take' of Fiona Richmond removing her knickers.

By now the audience was growing faintly uneasy and the casualty in the first row was bleeding quietly into his shoe. My attempt to switch the presentation to flip-over charts was thwarted by the fact that my ex-secretary had packed into my luggage fifteen pieces of totally blank cardboard in a neat leather folder. The real charts were still in London.

At this point, I surrendered to Murphy and suggested we break for coffee. As I left the platform I was approached by a small, wiry man with a military moustache who smelled faintly of Vick Vapour Rub and Gerber's baby food. 'Do you realize', he announced amiably, 'that your zip has broken?'

I glanced down. It had. Irrevocably. Now it is not easy to engage thirty or so pharmacists in casual bantering conversation when your shirt-tail is poking out of your fly, but I did make the attempt. Whether or not it was a successful attempt only history will tell. Suffice to say, my performance that day was at least unforgettable.

Another hazard of presentation is what appears to be the inevitable failure of sound equipment. Microphones, particularly of the lollipop variety, always seem to be covered with fluff or worse, and when switched on give off a dense crackling sound. I firmly believe that British Rail station announcers have a hand in this mischief, because the speaker's opening remarks will come out as 'Good . . . wheeze . . . ladies and grrrr-pop-scrunch . . . and welcome to the zzzzzzzz . . . splosh seminar'.

Loudspeakers are worse. Have you noticed how they whine with a frenzied intensity until you think your eardrums will burst? It never happens at rehearsals. Ever.

Which brings me to Turner's first law. 'If at all possible invite your audience to the rehearsal. It will go like a Swiss watch.'

There is also a remarkable piece of equipment on the market that looks just like a suitcase. You plonk it on the client's desk, snap open the catches and presto! A kind of video screen appears. You press another button and moving pictures leap into life, accompanied by razor-sharp sound. A boon for salesmen. Undoubtedly a major marketing tool for busy admen . . .

Except that a friend of mine, who must remain nameless, went to visit a client, who must also remain nameless, in Gosforth Park, Newcastle, and whipped his suitcase out on to the client's desk, confident that his five-minute video show would have them reeling in admiration. Well, you've probably guessed it, he'd brought the wrong case and as the lid fell open, two pairs of socks, a string vest and a copy of *Forum* spilled out on to the client's lap. It scarcely needs saying that a thorough check of your presentation aids before you have real, live, breathing clients in front of you is golden rule *numero uno*.

Multivisual presentations can, of course, be enormously impressive. It is the dream of most salesmen, certainly mine, to stand before a packed and adulatory throng at the Hollywood Bowl and give them a dazzling display of virtuosity using 35mm slides, back projection on a cinemascope screen, ten TV monitors, six Sony machines, giant flip-charts and quadrophonic sound. The entire presentation would, of course, be accompanied by live, nude, Afghanistan chartered accountants on silent roller skates.

Being serious for a moment, I do think presenters should avoid overkill. Colour slides, for example, may be ideal for a smallish audience, but can spell disaster if the larger audience can't read what's on them.

Turner's Law mark two says, 'Go to the very back of the hall yourself before the presentation, and if there is just one slide you can't read instantly and easily, snatch it up, take it outside and trample it underfoot.' Be ruthless with sound equipment. Beg or bribe the resident sound engineer, if he exists, to let you run through all the volume levels the day before your performance and pick the one that suits your voice.

If on the day itself your neck-mike fails, don't fiddle with it. Switch the bloody thing off and project your voice. If you can't project your voice, you shouldn't be up there mumbling in the first place.

If you use the modern slide projector with its facility for fading out your slides, a particularly attractive improvement on the old click-snap-jerk variety, do try to memorize where all the control buttons are. Nothing infuriates an audience more than a ceaseless blur of gently fading slides which blend into each other like soup.

If you must use statistics, use them sparingly, and never overfill your slide. Better to use three to get your point across than one that looks like a page torn from *Exchange and Mart*.

The most intimate presentation aid for me, apart from having my hand held by Lee Remick, is the 3M overhead projector. Dead easy to use, material can be prepared minutes before the presentation and it's ideally suited for small, boardroom-type meetings with only a limited group of people.

The best presentation I ever saw, using a battery of audiovisual aids so complex as to defy imagination, was given by the Ford Motor Company in the United States to a group of their dealers. It had everything, including five presenters, and was stage-managed with the precision of a Broadway musical.

It cost, I was reliably informed, over $50,000 to put together. So be warned. If you get flash, or just over-ambitious, you can spend money like water. It's not strictly necessary of course. Not everybody is impressed by technology. Don't let your audiovisual aids obscure your message. After all, it's *you* the presenter they've come to hear. Isn't it? I've seen many a marvellous message mangled by an overindulgence of hardware. Pick an aid you feel confident with and stick to it. Better by far to stand alone on the platform and talk unaided than be upstaged by Machiavellian machinery.

Finally, be of good cheer; one day soon the engineering profession will come up with a TV set that doesn't make pictures wobble like jelly, microphones that don't make your voice sound as if it's coming from inside a biscuit tin and a slide projector that is guaranteed jam-free. In the meantime, however, just check your zip before you get up on that platform.

16. Meetings and How to Cope with Them

The art of 'conspicuous invisibility'

Domination by sleight of hand and other vile, but indispensable tricks

Capturing the 'speech initiative'

For the purposes of this chapter we shall define meetings as those occasions when a salesman and at *least* two others are present to discuss business.

Meetings are a growth industry – as anybody who has ever tried to phone an important client knows. I should like a new penny for every time I have been told 'He's in a meeting'. The pile of money I would have accumulated in twenty-five years would probably circumnavigate the Isle of Wight with a few bob to spare.

Clearly, such a vital element in everyday business life must be mastered by the aspiring salestar. Very often a potential client will accept a 'meeting' with a salesman where the request for time to give a 'presentation' will be refused. Why? Well, a presentation can sound faintly intimidating. It smacks of a one-sided dialogue with charts and visual aids and, perhaps most important of all, unlike a 'meeting' it cannot be terminated until it has run its preordained time span.

The ritual of the meeting requires *one* person to be the 'chairman' or meeting convener – and a salesman should never seek to assume that role *overtly*. Let the client or buyer act as the host, even if the meeting is on 'neutral' territory like an hotel or restaurant. It is possible to influence or even *control* a meeting without actually being in the chair.

Here are a few pointers as to how this can be achieved.

Pre-meeting checklist

1. Identify and establish your own objectives. What do *you* want to achieve from the meeting?

2. Assess the competition. Are the others at the meeting heavy- or lightweight?

3. Should you adopt a passive or active role?

4. Are you fully equipped, both intellectually and psychologically, to face the potential *demands* of the meeting?

5. Arrive ahead of time. A coffee in reception ten minutes before the meeting starts will give you time to assess the atmosphere of the company.

   Is the receptionist cool, aloof, unfriendly? If she is, it is a *sure* indicator that you are dealing with a *formal*, possibly stuffy company. If she is pleasant, forthcoming and chatty you may glean important clues about the management style. If she tears off her whalebone corset and pounces on your body with a wild choking cry, are you *sure* you're in the right place? And if you are – you've certainly blown your chances of making a sale anyway.

At the meeting

1. Always remain *cool*. Anger and frustration – however justified – are strictly out of order.

2. Controlled amazement or incredulity – when finely honed – is OK. 'A return on capital employed of 117.9 per cent! I am amazed and impressed, Mr Stuntington-

Bladder, I really am!' And you would be, wouldn't you?

3. Always sit to attention, *never* slouch. *Body language* is important – nobody will take you seriously if you look like a damp sack of rotting artichokes that have just collapsed off the back of a lorry.

4. Tone of voice must be conciliatory. If you shout you threaten. Be cool.

5. Two people cannot speak at the same time for more than ten seconds. If this happens, give way *graciously*. Remember, *they are buying* – even though you know you are really selling.

   When the person who has overlapped your pitch finally pauses for breath then you can move in – and once you have captured the 'speech initiative' you must learn to retain it.

   Thus, long pauses for thought should be avoided – Nature abhors a vacuum, remember – speak steadily and calmly and if you detect an interruption looming it *can be deflected by the simple raising of a hand*. Try it. Palms uppermost, elbow slightly bent and do it with a smile – *but don't stop speaking*.

6. Notwithstanding the above, be a good listener. Nod sympathetically. Even the occasional controlled gasp is permissible.

   Never yawn. That is death. Unless you can develop the technique mastered by Frank Muir during his BBC days of yawning with your mouth shut. Beware, though – it's not easy. The planes of the face distort making you look like a plastic bag filled with rivets.

7. Remember that a man or woman's name is, to them, the most important thing they are ever likely to hear. *And they will never grow tired of hearing it.*

8. But for God's sake get it right. Addressing Mr Hartington as Mr Huntingdon may not sound like too

much of a *faux pas* but to Mr Hartington you might just as well have called him Jack the Ripper. Or Glenda.

9. Don't *argue*. Negotiate. Remember, you can *win* an argument and still lose the sale.

10. As you begin your cunningly disguised sales pitch *always open with a couple of uncontroversial statements* that your client *must* agree with. Get *him* used to saying *yes*. Frequently.

11. The word 'no' is a no-no.

12. Ration your physical gestures. A lot of arm-waving and table-thumping betrays an exhausted mind. Use the telling nod or meaningful shrug. Picking up and pointing with a pen is a useful piece of 'gamesmanship' *but it must be a decent pen*. Chewed biros are *out*.

    The crisp shuffling of documents can also convey authority. The dropping of them on the floor is not helpful. Neither is the balancing of the hot coffee on the lap. Great sales opportunities have been squandered by the 'scalded genitals syndrome'.

13. Only smoke if *they* do. And then *only* if you're a smoker. And avoid tearing the burning tip off the end of your fag between two fingers – the stench of incinerated flesh is not conducive to good business.

14. If the client farts – *don't laugh*.

15. If *you* fart, don't look round mysteriously as if it came from outer space – treat it like a sneeze or a cough, apologize *briefly* and *press on*.

16. Better still, *don't* fart at all.

17. Or belch.

18. Smile though. Lots. And *warmly*. Remember what I said in an earlier chapter: nobody buys anything from a misery guts.

19. You can *dominate* a meeting by sleight of hand. When the *senior* man is speaking, you must be all attention and all ears. Nodding throughout with a sincere expression is an excellent tactic.

20. Nodding *off*, isn't.

21. When the junior man speaks, *listen* – but *keep glancing back at the senior man* to assess *his* reaction. If he meets your eye, smile handsomely. If he greets his colleague's diatribe with what the Americans call an 'eye groan', respond with an *indulgent but world-weary smile*. This will establish common ground. You are now virtually blood brothers. When it's his turn to speak he'll know you're an ally.

22. If your client is a woman with nice legs, *avoid staring* at them. An approving glance is OK. Leering, winking and the smacking of the lips is *out*.

23. Jokes. If told at all they should be used sparingly. If the client chooses to tell one, laugh politely but don't go overboard and writhe helplessly on the floor – he won't be convinced.

24. Always leave when you 'sense' the meeting has run its course. The pointers are fairly easy to discern – client yawns, glances at watch, buzzes for secretary, takes phone calls, shuffles papers impatiently, looks wistfully out of window, dies of a sudden heart seizure.

25. After you've left – and *before* you go out on the next call – jot down any salient points of action you must take. If you've promised to check a fact, supply more data, send a sample, etc., *make bloody sure you do*.

    Finally, on your way out, thank the secretary or receptionist for coffee etc., and leave her/him with a smile and a warm feeling. Remember, to her you're just traffic – try to make your brief visit a shade more indelible than the rest.

What about internal meetings on your home patch back at headquarters? How should you conduct yourself through these elaborately mined and delicately balanced fields of fire? The first thing to remember about *internal* meetings is that you must still *behave like a salesman*. It doesn't matter that you are on familiar terms with your supervisor, your sales manager or the vice-chairman. Be on your mettle, present the image of yourself you are most keen to establish with your superiors *at all times*.

If your internal meeting is attended by *other salesmen* you have got to treat it as a *competitive situation*. Selling yourself *inwards* is what the Americans call it. And the rules are pretty tough. First of all, some don'ts.

1. *Don't* reveal your 'good idea' to other salesmen before your meeting with the boss. They'll cannibalize it so fast you'll smell burning rubber.

2. *Don't* be the last one to join the meeting, and don't drift in with the herd.

3. *Don't* show up in shirt sleeves with your tie loosened, even if it's hot. Force yourself to *look* cool, businesslike and *ready for anything*.

4. *Don't* listen to other salesmen's moans. Make your own list of items you want to raise – be *different*, you're *not* one of the boys. Are you? Not in front of the boss you're not – *you* are the salesman who is still at his desk when the others are in the pub boasting and whining. (Have you noticed *that's* what salesmen *do* in pubs?)

Now a few dos:

1. *Do* try and be first in the room when your boss calls a meeting. Even a couple of minutes will *establish*, eventually, that you are a keen frontrunner.

2. Bring all the necessary paperwork with you. If you anticipate being asked why Fotheringay's Emporium reduced their monthly order with you then *be certain to have a convincing answer ready*.

3. *Volunteer* information. Make helpful suggestions. *Welcome* new sales targets. But don't be a *creep*. If you disagree – *speak up*. But without rancour.

4. *Be attentive*. Oh, I know that sounds crass, but nothing pisses a sales director off more resoundingly than one of his flock looking out of the window, glancing at his watch or whispering asides to colleagues.

5. If you have a special request, or a piece of really powerful information to impart, wait until the others have gone. You want the boss to give you his undivided attention, don't you?

If a colleague attempts to upstage you, or ridicule some point you are making – *beware*. The boss will form a specific view of you depending on how you react. So if Reg Needlethorpe from the northern sales office puts you down with a sarcastic remark, don't rise to the bait.

Men and women of authority can field criticism without losing a moment's cool. Have you noticed how the most polished political performers on television deal with rude hecklers? They *never* descend to the same level of abuse, and neither should you. Remember, your boss will be watching exchanges between his sales team like an umpire at a tennis tournament. He can learn a lot about you by observing your performance under stress.

Later in the pub, of course, you can tell Reg Needlethorpe that he is a pathetic wally with a brain small enough to fit into the corner of a thimble. But do it with a weary smile.

Best of all you should avoid *too much fraternization* with other salesmen in the same company. This can prove to be difficult. We all develop friendships at work, but if you are to be a *superstar* you *have* to accept that such friendships are transitory and you will be moving *onwards* and *upwards* like a nuclear-fuelled rocket.

Finally, remember that *all* meetings whether internal or external are *potential battlefields*. Your performance, your style, your powers of persuasion and your *future* success can all be on the line, even at the most mundane gathering.

Resolve to *outshine* the competition *internally* and to become the *trusted advocate* and *counsellor externally*. Make your customers and your boss *need* you – make it easy for them to *rely* on you and you will have sunk powerful roots from which to grow to superstar proportions. This last piece of advice is vital.

17. A Connoisseur's Guide to Conferring in Comfort

It is not a widely appreciated fact among British marketing folk that there is a special conference held every three years for antique salesmen (that is to say, vendors of antique objects rather than eighty-year-old, clapped-out reps), and the venue for this esoteric event is Cairo – where else?

I happened to be in Egypt in 1978 when this most serious gathering of marketing specialists was taking place. I was regrettably unable to register as a last-minute delegate (for tax purposes, you understand) since the organizers seemed rather sceptical about my credentials. 'Just how old are these advertising minutes you claim you sell?' asked a man looking suspiciously like Omar Sharif. Unable, as usual, to bluff or dissemble, I had to admit I was on holiday and that my interest in the Great Pyramid of Cheops was no more than cursory.

The Sharif doppelgänger turned away with a sneer and closed the tent flap behind him. Beyond the silken walls, still bathed in shafts of desert sunlight, I could hear the click and whirr of a slide projector and the muffled applause of numberless delegates as they were held in thrall by a dissertation on the art of maximizing the market share for eighteenth-dynasty scarabs bearing the royal seal of Tutankhamen, the boy king.

Thus rejected, I consoled myself with a light luncheon of camel's hoof soup and a handful of Diocalm tablets. pondering throughout on the vagaries of commercial life. Across the whole surface of the globe, I pondered conferences of one sort or another were actually taking place. In Manchester and Katmandu, Peru and Moose Jaw, Nantucket and Omsk, men and women wearing little badges were sitting in darkened halls trying to keep their eyelids from clamping shut, while above them on raised platforms men with their nostrils illuminated from below rabbited on about cash-flow projections and inflation accounting.

It seemed to me then, and I have had no reason to change my view since, that there ought to be a set of rough ground rules for attending seminars in foreign parts.

First of all, and perhaps inevitably, one should select a conference that actually interests you professionally. Exotic locations can be a snare for the unwary. I mean to say, even Shangri-la palls if you have to absorb a four-day crash course on the laminated rivet industry, especially if, on the last night (always mysteriously called 'Gala' evenings), you are required to put on a dinner jacket and dance with the local mayor's wife.

Incidentally, local mayors always insist on making forty-minute speeches in fractured English on how splendid it is for you to select their town for your deliberations. And their wives always suffer from what seems like terminal halitosis.

Having selected a subject that will enrich your store of knowledge and your company's, try and check out the hotels at which delegates will be expected to stay. This is no trivial matter. In my experience it is better to endure say, Oldham, in a first-class hotel, than Paris in a hideous plastic funnel, designed for dwarf Japanese tourists. Such a place exists, I assure you! If your own funds run to it, try and opt out of the rotten old conference hotel and pay the extra to stay close at hand, but in some style and luxury. In Paris, rather than suffer the kamikaze matchbox to which I have already referred, I set up in the magnificent L'Hôtel on the Left Bank where bar prices were cheaper anyway.

Once happily located, and with one's Gucci suitcase unpacked, make a careful study of the delegate list. Mark with red felt-pen those people who must be avoided at all costs. This will not be easy as very boring delegates are a special breed who have a habit of catching you off guard during the tea break and bludgeoning you into joining them for dinner at 'a little restaurant the locals use' – which invariably turns out to be an overheated slum stuffed with fat American tourists in Bermuda shorts who discuss their varicose veins loudly over plates of steaming, rancid pasta.

Always go to the opening session. Here you can survey the assembled throng and make plans to approach those delegates who can either be of value to you commercially (and people are more approachable in foreign countries for some obscure reason), or those who might make congenial companions for the three-day visit. Don't be ashamed to hustle. No delegate has any right to object if you want to talk business. What the hell are they there for anyway? (OK! Answers on a postcard to the Cedars of Lebanon Alcoholic Hospital, Nantwich, Near Tibet, please.)

Make dates with people who would normally be difficult to see in England. The President of the World Bank, for example. He always refuses to see me when he's in London. Next time we're together at a conference in Bavaria I'll nail him, just you wait and see.

During the actual conference sessions – you know, those things that take place while everybody else is boozing and running spiritedly along golden beaches – do try and be the guy to ask the speaker a really difficult question like, 'In relation to your penultimate chart showing the macroeconomic trends in the bottled hen's ovaries market, could you please relate it to the incidence of bulk buying among hunchback supermarket owners in a recessionary cycle underpinned by artificially low interest rates?'

This kind of question always makes them think. Just occasionally it results in you being offered a job by a research company, or alternatively, being dragged outside and beaten unconscious with a chair leg.

Phone the office every day. Yes, every day. Apart from making your secretary feel wanted, it does impress those sceptics in England who believe that all overseas visits are little short of drug-crazed orgies.

Before enquiring about how things are at home base, drop a few hints about murky weather, bad plumbing, outbreaks of plague, damp beds and relentless hard work. Never admit to enjoying yourself. Except when phoning from Huddersfield, which does, of course, qualify as 'overseas' in my book at least. From the Grand Scimitar Hotel in that self-same northern town you must exude over the telephone an impression of sensual abandon so Carthaginian as to be almost beyond comprehension. Let slip casual references to topless dentists, nude karate lessons in lukewarm treacle, fabulous restaurants hidden behind the Co-op, and most important of all, that among the surprise speakers are David Ogilvy, Lord Leverhulme, Milton Friedman and Jane Fonda.

Always keep copies of the various papers that are presented at an overseas conference. Some day you'll be asked to speak and it's amazing how useful recycled monologues on plastic extrusions can be, even if they are five years old.

Take a wife with you. If your own won't go, somebody else's will have to suffice. Many invitations or items on the 'social programme' involve the ladies. You don't want to miss a tour of that glass-blowing factory again, do you? Make a serious list of things you hope to achieve by attending the conference. Yes, a serious list. You may wish to expand your contacts, meet those marketing directors from Slough who have proved so difficult to reach throughout the year. You may wish to use some of the material on offer in your next sales pitch back in England.

Soak up as much knowledge as you possibly can and always try to learn at least three 'buzz' words per day. I first heard 'media dynamics' uttered in Madrid seven years ago and now I use it constantly. Nobody asks me what it means, thank God, but it does impress when injected into a lengthy pitch about television overlap statistics.

Follow up those casual meetings in the sun lounge where

the marketing whizzkid of some up-and-coming company promised to test his new product with your TV station/ magazine/store/bus-side. Ring the fellow immediately you return home.

Go and do a store check in the local supermarket. See how it's done in Acapulco, Rome, Zurich, Haiti. Watch out for products that may arrive in the UK months later having cut their teeth in foreign markets. Knowledge is strength. If you are a media man and you see a new pack from a familiar stable make a note of it and try an early bid for the business before it lifts off in Granadaland under an assumed name. (Did you know that Krona margarine was once called Fairy? Try spreading that on your wholemeal toast, buster!)

If you're a brand manager, steal foreign ideas without a blush of shame. Look at packaging, pricing, design, shop layout – everything in fact. And do try to attend at least half the conference sessions too. If you plan your intinerary carefully you won't get an attack of the guilts on the last day when that nifty redhead suggests a spot of hang-gliding followed by bird's nest soup at her place.

Never use cash. Don't get drunk. Eat sensibly, and if in the Middle East, not at all! Last, but not least, don't forget your passport and do try to remember that a car parked at Heathrow for five days with the side lights on tends not to be much use when your delayed flight deposits you at the airport at three in the morning.

18. The Hazards of Executive Travel

It is an established fact that your average nine-to-five deskbound office worker feels nothing but pity for those people like myself whose work requires them to travel in jet planes, boats, trains and even cablecars in pursuit of a humble living wage.

I have often pondered this fact while sipping Dom Perignon high above the Atlantic between London and New York and it therefore seems appropriate, if not actually overdue, for me to set down in print some of the hazards of sales executive travel in this latter part of the twentieth century. Let us start, as all journeys have to, by road.

Few salesmen, even junior ones, actually travel to business meetings by charabanc, although the airport bus is just acceptable as a means to an end. The end, of course, is the airport itself, a place that sometimes seems to suggest that it was invented solely to increase the tensions and bad temper of the travelling salesman. The first thing that should be understood is that airports are very similar indeed to hospitals. In both places one is at the mercy of nameless officials who possess knowledge and, above all, superior power, over those hapless fools who chance to be their customers. Thus, discipline and order are paramount and woe betide the man or woman who tries to buck the system. Except, gentle reader, bucking the system actually works!

Let me explain: I fly on average once a month, sometimes more, and over the years I have established that the 'check-in' times can safely be ignored. It is tyrannical to be required to show up at an airport one hour before your flight is due to leave. All that happens if you do display this punctuality is that you are cast upon the mercy of airport officials who, smiling wolfishly, will shunt you from departure lounge to departure lounge, scrutinizing your ticket as if you've just forged it, and then, when the plane is due to take off at last, tell you it is to be delayed for forty minutes.

As a rough guideline, therefore, arrival half an hour before scheduled take-off time is adequate. If travelling by British Airways, as I usually do, three minutes might well be ample, as it is the quaint tradition of our native airline to aim at a kind of ritual lateness of departure. Never be upset if your flight is delayed. Expect it. Then on those blessed and rare occasions when you do take off promptly, it can be looked upon as a special treat or bonus.

Never enquire as to why your flight is delayed. Especially if the reason shouted in muffled tones over the loudspeaker suggests that it is 'technical'. Unless, of course, you happen to be in Malta. Once at Malta Airport I asked to be told specifically just what 'technical' hitch had caused our delay, and the British Airways crew member, courteous to the last, virtually frogmarched me to the front of the plane where a Maltese engineer with a tobacco tin, filled with curtain rings and tiny rivets, was holding an incomprehensible conversation with the captain. I gathered that a bit had dropped off and it was just a question of replacing it. Reassured by the crew's smiling confidence, I remained on the steps by the open aircraft door and took the sun for an hour, while the rest of the passengers almost expired in their seats through lack of air conditioning.

On another occasion some years ago I was on a charter flight to Reims in northern France with an old friend, Stewart McAlpine, Chairman of Smedley McAlpine Advertising. We had been conducting urgent business with the Taittinger Champagne people and after a gruelling day, relieved only by a six-course gourmet lunch and seven gallons of pink bubbly, we repaired to the airfield at Reims for the journey home. Only minutes after our ancient charter plane started its engines, it was discovered that the old heap simply wasn't capable of making the sharp left turn necessary to actually get it on the airstrip ready for take-off. I felt a twinge of pity for the pilot when he shamefacedly explained that we were stuck. My pity evaporated rather quickly when he then suggested that all male passengers get off and push! Ridiculous though it may sound, we did just that. How many other salesmen have pushed an aircraft thirty yards to position it for take-off? My advice on cheap, charter flights, therefore, is to wear strong overalls and carry a supply of surgical trusses. You can always pack your Austin Reed executive suit in your luggage and change in your client's loo. If he has one.

For long-distance flights, scheduled airlines are by far the best bet and notwithstanding my earlier remarks, I am a keen user of British Airways. Frequently on the transatlantic run I meet fascinating and famous people. I once sat next to the delectable Leslie Caron on a flight from Los Angeles. She fell asleep.

On another occasion between London and New York I shared first class with David Frost. I fell asleep.

On yet a third occasion my travelling companion was a famous lady stripper, renowned for her libidinous generosity. Everybody else on the plane fell asleep.

A word about baggage may be appropriate here! If possible, on the short-haul journeys, take only hand luggage. This can speed up the boring formalities at your destination quite dramatically. Never buy expensive luggage. It's simply sitting there asking to be nicked. And never, ever, put any files in your main suitcase which relate to meetings you are due to attend. All such papers should be in your briefcase on your lap. You can always replace lost pyjamas, jockstraps and toothbrushes in New York or Peru, but never vital company documents. Generally, I travel as lightly as possible, although once, I will confess, I took my dirty laundry to Los Angeles because they do such a superb job on it at the Beverly Hills Hotel. Ropey old shirts with frayed cuffs were returned packed in cellophane boxes just like brand new.

What to do during those long journeys? Well, if you aren't lucky enough to have a nubile travelling companion, you could try working. There are distinct advantages: you are not interrupted by the telephone or members of staff seeking pay rises or even secretaries claiming to have been raped by the chief accountant. Meals are served on time, if you like plastic chicken that is, and you, the traveller, can toil busily at your five-year sales plan, secure in your silver bullet high above the earth's atmosphere.

What if flying scares the living daylights out of you? Well, that's tough and there's no known cure, except arriving at the departure lounge blind drunk and unconscious. I love flying and find it exhilarating. I once went on to the flight deck of Concorde and looked at all the controls. It's got to be the most amazing thing since crutchless tights, believe me.

Because of my enthusiasm for flying, I actually prefer light aircraft where you can experience all the nuances of hurtling through space in a tube of metal with wings – flying in fog or driving snow without instruments, for example, makes any journey that much more exhilarating!

Not all sales trips are to glamorous destinations, of course, and to demonstrate just how serious an executive traveller I am, I will admit that I regularly visit Manchester and Birmingham.

Oddly enough, my brief experiences with the Heathrow-Manchester shuttle have always been something of a nightmare. Only recently, accompanied by two colleagues, I drove from Westbourne Grove to Heathrow in about sixteen minutes in order to catch a connection crucial to our first meeting in Manchester. As we hurtled up the ramp to Terminal One, exhaust pluming, tyres howling, I realized that we would just make the flight by the skin of our teeth. I was so exhilarated at this victory of human endeavour over time and space that I disgorged my colleagues and roared off to the nearby car park with their luggage still locked in my boot. I still think buying them both new Tesco shirts and disposable toothbrushes in Manchester was an act of wild over-compensation.

Of course, aeroplanes can only take you so far. Getting from the airport to your actual destination offers a wide variety of choice, the cheapest being the faithful old airport bus. This is all you need in civilized places like Paris and New York, but they are to be avoided like the plague in Cairo and Istanbul. Unless, of course, you actually enjoy sharing the interminable journey with live poultry, drunken soldiers with loaded carbines, and fat old women in black dresses who surreptitiously pick their noses.

Taxis vary, and in most foreign countries it is wise to agree a firm price *before* the journey commences. Even in Geneva such a precaution is to be recommended. A cabby there once tried to charge me £35 for the fifteen-minute journey from airport to La Réserve Hotel. I refused and suggested he go away and perform an impossible physical act with himself. Instead he relented, and we settled for eleven quid, but it was still pricey!

Never catch a taxi in Moscow. It is part of the Communist world plan to kill off English capitalists by poisoning them with the garlic breath of their taxi drivers. In Paris, use nothing but taxis! Only they can survive the horrors of French traffic, unless you go by Métro, but then you'll probably end up engaged, pregnant or a member of the Foreign Legion.

In Los Angeles, hire a car. The only pedestrians there are bums, rapists and nuns on marathon charity walks. The Californians are really tuned into the motorcar age and renting a car there is simplicity itself. My first trip to Hollywood some years ago was packed with incident. Within an hour of getting off the plane at Los Angeles Airport I had hired a Ford Thunderbird, hit a parked car in Beverly Hills, torn its door off, and argued with the owner. I was rescued by a young traffic cop who exonerated me from all blame and then given a fresh car by Hertz who didn't even expect me to apologize!

Things are different in New York City. Ten years ago, in my dazzling youth, I tried to enter the subway near Broadway on 71st Street wearing a dinner suit – I'd been to the theatre with friends. A New York cop, who would have made Kojak seem like Enid Blyton, told me to 'scram and catch a cab'. Only later was I informed that he had done it for my own protection: any twit foolish enough to get on the New York Subway at midnight in a dinner jacket would be mugged and robbed. Not *maybe*. *Would* be. Remember that, the next time you totter across Leicester Square after a hearty supper at Terrazza, and be grateful for England's small mercies.

Generally speaking, I'm a lucky traveller, but I do acknowledge that some people are dogged by misfortune. Another old friend of mine, Herb Liebovitz, now living in New York, only had to step on an aircraft and bits started falling off on to the runway.

I have the same effect on trains. They don't like me, nor me them. The only possible exception I will make is the Orient Express which runs between London and Venice. All the others are a disaster. I have the same effect on them as a Mafia kiss of death. How many other travellers can better my record of eleven hours, eighteen minutes between Paddington and Plymouth? Without a restaurant car *and* unflushable toilets? Oh yes, we executive jet-setters have to be made of stern stuff, not least of all when travelling by British Rail.

Finally, and prosaically, let me recommend my favourite mode of travel in central London when weather permits. Yes, you've guessed it, you clever devils – it's walking. When you've slept at supersonic speeds, hovered in helicopters, bobbed in boats, trembled in trains and cursed in cabs, it makes a nice change to use your legs. Besides which it's a lot better for your constitution.

19. Expenses

The invisible line between prudence and profligacy

Are your expenses really necessary?

All salesmen incur expenses in the legitimate pursuit of business. Sending a representative out on the road without adequate financial support is like trying to drive across the Kalahari Desert on half a gallon of petrol. You won't achieve your objective.

Expenses, therefore, are an inescapable fact of commercial life even though the mere mention of them does more than anything else to raise feelings of jealousy, suspicion and anguish among those whose work precludes them from claiming. One man's legitimate expense – goes the saying – is another man's tax-free handout. And the size and the *nature* of expense accounts vary so enormously as to be two almost entirely separate points on a vast and sometimes dazzling spectrum.

The junior rep who makes his ten calls a day on foot in the East End of London may consider himself lucky to reclaim a few pounds a week on bus and tube fares, whereas the international businessman in hot pursuit of a large contract may find himself legitimately incurring considerable sums of money to secure his objectives. Expenses themselves are neither 'good' nor 'bad'. They are neutral.

What *is* important is the way in which the salesman who is privileged to qualify for them actually deploys them as a business resource. Expense accounts breed self-confidence. They are the lubrication that makes the wheels of commerce turn more smoothly and efficiently and they cause a whole series of unexpectedly beneficial side-effects. Many great hotels and restaurants throughout the world can only exist because of expense-account spending. Some economies, notably the Japanese, seem to revolve almost entirely around the expense-account principle.

First and foremost, therefore, let us remind ourselves of the Inland Revenue's rather chilling definition of what constitutes a legitimate expense: it is something that is incurred 'wholly, exclusively and necessarily in the performance of the duties of a businessman's office or employment'.

Have you got that? Wholly, exclusively and necessarily.

For the young salesman who is given his first expense account there are a few common-sense rules which will help him to cope with the awesome responsibility of spending somebody else's money. Expenses fall into many categories, but there are two areas which need identifying.

1. **The Unavoidable Expense**
2. **The Optional Expense**

Here are some examples.

Unavoidable	*Optional*
Travel expenses (train, bus, plane, taxi)	Entertaining
	Car hire
Minimum hotel accommodation away from home	Business gifts
Phone calls to base from sales territory	

The individual salesman *knows* what his unavoidable expenses are and they rarely cause anguish among the chartered accountant fraternity back at head office . . . unless of course he claims the taxi fare from London Bridge to Piccadilly is £98.73, plus gratuity. It is in fact a bit less than that!

Where the salesman has to tread carefully is in the area of

optional expense. A good sales manager will lay down the guidelines *clearly* before the salesman goes out and makes a fool of himself. In some trades 'entertaining' is deliberately avoided or severely restricted. In others it is part of the culture. Some companies provide credit cards for their sales team and others don't, believing that they encourage overspending, even profligacy. There is some merit in this view.

I usually spend more on 'private' purchases when I use my own credit card – the chances are I would do the same if I had a 'company' card.

It is a good discipline to spend hard cash and then reclaim it, but these days carrying large sums of money isn't always a sensible thing to do. The salesman should always keep a copy of his expenses, even after they have been approved and paid by his company. The gentlemen of the Inland Revenue still have a right to ask penetrating questions about that business trip to Borneo, where you and your wife entertained the British Commercial Attaché to a nine-course meal accompanied by dancing head hunters and four gallons of vintage Moët et Chandon. And they will. Believe me.

So, keep good, clear records. Make a note of what you spend *every* day. Don't trust your memory. Nothing is worse than sitting down at the end of the month and scratching your head over just *where* that £300 actually went. Itemize as much detail as possible. It's a good discipline and it makes accountants a lot less nervous.

I once knew a flamboyant businessman who submitted an account that read:

To general entertaining in April/May   £3325

There were no further details. No breakdown of events. No receipts. No bills. He had a rather difficult time getting paid.

When buying lunch – by far the biggest single item on most salesmen's expense accounts – make sure you check the bill carefully. Restaurants have a funny tendency to get their arithmetic wrong when they know you are not paying out of your own pocket.

Watch the VAT and 15 per cent service trick as well. Some restaurants give you bills which state – in small print – 'Prices include VAT and 15 per cent service'. People should be careful not to add *another* tip. Also, the service should be on the *pre*-VAT total – if there is one. Not to mention the deliberate gap at the bottom of a credit card bill when the meal prices are listed as 'service included'. Many a salesman in a hurry has added another 15 per cent to a bill that is already heavily loaded with extras. If a restaurant advertises a set-price lunch which seems reasonable, watch the 'add-ons' like a hawk. Six pounds a head for a three-course meal may seem stunningly attractive in a fancy establishment situated in a good part of town, until you realize that rolls and butter are two quid a throw and mineral water five quid a bottle.

Beware also of the hotelier who leaves a welcoming ice-bucket of champagne in your room when you arrive. *It isn't always with his compliments.* I fell for this some years ago and had to engage in a furious argument with the cashier on checking-out day. 'But I thought it was free,' I protested. The cashier, certain she was out of earshot, whispered, 'Look darling, in this hotel nothing's free.' I have remembered her words ever since.

The very first hotel I was required to stay in on expenses was over thirty years ago in Brighton. As far as I know it may still exist so I'd better not use its real name. It was a classic 'traveller's' hotel which specialized in the transient, foot-weary brigade of confectionery reps, insurance salesmen and baked bean hawkers. It was small, dingy and overwhelmingly depressing. The walls were covered with dark brown wallpaper and the floors with threadbare coconut matting. A faint odour of cabbage water hung in all the rooms and it was permanently cold inside – even in summer.

Individual bedrooms were clearly designed for hunchback dwarfs, with only enough space to open the door and squeeze in past the brass bedstead. In order to save on fuel bills, the proprietor, a rat-faced cynic who had a cigarette dangling permanently from his lower lip, only fitted extremely low-wattage bulbs in all the lamps so that trying to read a paper was like an exercise in telepathy. You had to guess what was in the news.

The hotel's denizens were a sorry lot. Slightly overweight, ageing salesmen who had burnt themselves out in the service of vast grocery conglomerates who paid them pitiful wages and excruciatingly mean commissions.

Sitting in the residents' lounge – a fourteen-foot-square cell, furnished with frayed armchairs that would have disgraced a workhouse – I felt an overwhelming sense of despair and panic. *This* was expense-account living? Well, that was just one taste of it, and I suppose it was a salutary experience.

In addition to travel and hotel expenses a lot of salesmen these days are provided with a company car. The provision of a motor vehicle doesn't always mean that you need it 'wholly, exclusively and necessarily' to perform your duties. Many top managers enjoy the 'car perk' even though they hardly ever leave their desks.

Recent legislation has made the 'perk' less attractive than it was, and now differentiates between the 'car as a reward' and the 'car as a vital tool of the job'. This is fair.

If you're lucky enough to enjoy a company car, don't grumble if the tax man makes you cough up more than you did in the past. It's still a valuable thing to have – and much better than having the hassle of buying and maintaining your own vehicle. So pay up – and smile.

Always try to *anticipate* your expenses needs. If you know you have a series of big lunches for important clients all coming up in the same month, rearrange your future schedule so that any overspend on budget can be redeemed in the following month.

And try to avoid confusing your own personal spending with legitimate expenses. Or claiming you entertained a client last month who died two years ago. (You think I'm joking?!)

Business gifts? Are they a necessary evil? I believe they are dangerous unless part of official company policy. Many firms send out Easter eggs or desk diaries or monogrammed pens to favoured customers. So far so good. If, on the other hand, the salesman on the territory starts doling out boxes of crystallized fruit, theatre tickets or sexy underwear to his clients, he is in danger of creating a precedent. And he will find it very difficult to claim such expenses back from his company.

Better by far to treat your very special customer *personally* out of your own pocket. It keeps things very simple and you will have no difficult conversations with your chief accountant about items on the expense sheet that stands out like a sore thumb.

On a lighthearted note, my very favourite expenses story was about a young American salesman who was tempted on to the Alaska gaming tables during a business trip to the Frozen State. A surfeit of champagne made him a trifle reckless and he very soon lost a thousand dollars. Undaunted, he made out an expense claim the next day which read:

Lonely in Alaska, bought dog	$300
Dog lonely, bought bitch	$250
Dog ill, medical expenses	$250
Dog died, funeral expenses	$170

When the expense claim was submitted his chief accountant gloatingly pointed out that the total was $970 against an advance of $1000. The salesman whipped out his gold Parker pen and added the following line with a flourish:

Flowers for bereaved bitch	$30

I'd like to return, briefly, to the differences between expenses which are 'wholly, exclusively and necessarily' incurred on company business and those which are quite clearly a laundered form of remuneration.

We've touched on cars. *Sixty-five per cent* of British executives actually have company vehicles. Not all of them by any stretch of the imagination *need* them for the execution of their duties. At the slightly more esoteric end of the scale, we have 'corporate' Lear jets and 'company' penthouses used exclusively by one or two favoured executives.

The proliferation of such fringe benefits says a great deal more about our personal taxation system in this country than the meretriciousness of British tycoons.

Individual companies will formulate their own views about such extravagances, and they will vary enormously. If a salesman, for example, needs to travel both extensively and internationally in the legitimate pursuit of his duties, his hotels, meals, taxis and aeroplane expenses will be prodigious. This is *not* to say they aren't all totally justified. The *size* of the expenses incurred, therefore, should not be a criterion of judgement about the salesman's performance in the field.

There are cynics – I am reliably informed – who say that the bigger the claim, the less chance of its being queried by a Pecksniffian book-keeper back at the ranch. It is the petty items, like puncture repair outfits, corn plasters and parking meter expenses, that are vigorously challenged by accountants and their beady-eyed henchmen. *Apparent authenticity* is the key. If you keep meticulous records, you should have no trouble in convincing your company of the solidity of your case.

But take heed. If you work in a large company which employs many salesmen, beware of duplicated claims. Many years ago, I was selling advertising space for a large publishing conglomerate which, across all its titles, employed at least one hundred reps. The group advertisement director was a smooth, world-weary executive who had forgotten more expense-account dodges than most salesmen dream up in a lifetime. One Friday morning, he called a meeting of all the advertisement sales staff. On his desk in the big meeting room was a small pile of expense sheets and at his side stood the company's chief accountant, a man whose facial expression resembled that of a multiple rapist recently parachuted into a harem full of raving nymphomaniacs.

'I have in front of me', drawled the advertisement director, when we were all fearfully assembled, 'no less than *nineteen* salesmen's expense sheets. Each one of these salesmen claims to have bought Mr Basil Spice lunch last Friday.'

Here, the ad director paused and lit his usual Turkish cigarette. The atmosphere was tense. The salesman next to me scarcely suppressed a whimper.

'What this state of affairs clearly indicates', continued the director smoothly, 'is one of two things. Either Mr Basil Spice is a man of prodigious appetite, one might even say monumental greed, or – and this is the explanation that I am bound to say I find much more credible – *eighteen* of you gentlemen are telling me fibs.'

A kind of hysterical silence hung over the big conference room like an invisible mushroom cloud, as rows of salesmen desperately tried to remember what they'd written down on their expense sheets. The director enjoyed a few more moments of suspense and then invited the recalcitrant nineteen to step forward to repossess their expense sheets in order to, as he put it, 'redeploy their flagging imaginations and failing memories'.

Some considerable time later – it may well have been a year or more – I met with the same Mr Basil Spice who was a famous and much-loved advertising-space buyer for an advertising agency in London. I relayed this chilling tale – even supplying him with the date on which the nineteen alleged lunches took place. Being an efficient and well-organized man, he returned to his office and located his old diary. After scrutinizing it, he phoned me back and said, 'Harry? This will slay you. On that particular day, *not one person* from your organization bought me as much as a lousy sausage roll – let alone nineteen lunches!'

I have never forgotten that cautionary tale. The lesson is clear. If more than *one* salesman in the *same* company is likely to call on or entertain the *same* client – for God's sake, compare notes *before* you bung in your expense sheets!

If you are about to embark on a long business trip abroad, try to persuade your company to establish a line of credit for you in the countries you are to visit – or arrange for a travel agent to act as principal on your behalf so that you only need to sign the hotel bills when you check out. Many a sales trip has been wrong-footed by lost traveller's cheques, stolen cash or, worst of all, denial of credit facilities.

If in doubt about what constitutes a legitimate expense (e.g., will the company pay for my haircut in Sri-Lanka before that vital meeting?), ask your boss. If he won't commit himself, use your imagination. You're a salesman, aren't you?

If you were a chief accountant in another life (sorry about this), which of the following expense claims would raise your disapproving hackles as they flopped on to your desk for payment?

Expense Claim 'A'

	£
Taxi fares to station	3.50
Copy of *Penthouse* magazine to read on train	1.50
3 x gin and tonics for blonde with huge thighs in same compartment	2.80
Entrance fee to Saucy Kitty's nightclub in Huddersfield	5.00
Half a bottle of imitation champagne in nightclub with potential buyer, Mr A. J. Smith	28.00

Hush-money to cab driver who drove
   Mr A. J. Smith, drunk as a skunk, back to
   his dismal house in north Huddersfield   10.00

Damage to hostess's left fingernail in ensuing
   scuffle   2.00

Phone calls in hotel to wife, bookmaker,
   mistress and chiropodist   7.75
Total for trip   £60.55

Expense Claim 'B'

	£
Taxi fare to station via showrooms	6.50
Snack on train while planning presentation	5.00
Dinner with Mr A. J. Smith and wife	38.00
Use of secretarial services and gratuities at hotel	11.05
Total	60.55

Easy? Expense account 'A' doesn't have a prayer, does it? I mean to say, lusting after blondes on trains and nasty nightclubs and all the rest. Disgraceful! Whereas expense account 'B', while light on supporting vouchers and receipts, is pretty routine, isn't it? Except that expense account 'A' is a *true* description of how the money was spent and expense account 'B' is a tissue of lies!

Am I therefore advocating dishonesty? No, I am not. But it is a foolish salesman who can't so organize his expenses so as to keep both him and his accountant – *and* the tax man – reasonably happy.

So, good hunting.

20. Incentives

Do organizations give selling the importance it deserves?

Do you want to be rich and famous at last?

When I was a young, idealistic salesman flogging canned groceries to indifferent customers in hostile territory (Aldgate East) I nurtured a dream that one day I would work for an organization that recognized the true value of a really good sales team.

At the time of writing, this dream remains as strong as ever. In this sceptred isle the trade of selling – now fashionably called marketing – stands patiently in the wings waiting to be called into the spotlight in the centre of the stage. It is still faintly vulgar to many people. Salespeople are pushy . . . a bit emotional. They have inflated opinions of themselves and, when all is said and done, these qualities are, frankly old boy, rather un-British.

The present economic malaise, we are told by clever journalists in the posh Sunday papers, is due to lack of productivity. If only we could make more things our troubles would vanish almost as quickly as they arrived. Now, while I confess a bias against pretty well all economic journalists (fatuous theorists that they undoubtedly are), I also genuinely believe that a little more attention to selling, as opposed to simply manufacturing, would be a positive step in the right direction.

It's no coincidence that in the USA, the crucible of capitalist endeavour, some of the most successful companies on the face of the earth have been founded and run by old-fashioned, two-fisted salesmen. The hiring and subsequent motivation of hungry, goal-orientated salespeople has been at the root of their basic philosophy. Thomas Edison is quoted as having said, 'My salespeople are the highest earners in the company – they are the wealth producers.'

That view is not common around British boardroom tables. Commission earnings, for example, must have a ceiling. Why? Should profits have an artificial limit too? Speak to a random selection of chartered accountants – go on, force yourself – and they will tell you that in times of economic stress you should trim, cut back, penny-pinch, pull in your horns and all the other negative Pavlovian reactions which their flesh is heir to.

Now, while it is only good sense to run a lean, well-disciplined organization at all times, the way to punch out of an economic recession is to become greedy for increased sales: to become obsessed by the desire to carve out a bigger share of the market even if that same market is itself dwindling. The route to real success lies in aggressive marketing, coupled with a sound financial structure – not wielding the bloody axe. No cut-back ever produced a single extra sale. How could it?

Motivating a salesman, however, is much more likely to bolster income and profit, if the right targets are set and the right rewards available. Is money the only way to motivate a salesman? Obviously not. Work environment, good colleagues, inspired leadership, enthusiasm and faith in the product are all vital ingredients in the mix. But let's not be coy about it. Money is usually near, if not actually at the top of the list.

Should salesmen sincerely want to be rich? In my book, if they don't, what the hell are they doing in the business in the first place? If people are ashamed of success or affluence, they can always become priests, civil servants or Alaskan nudists – and the best of luck to them.

Back to motivation, however. *Cassells English Dictionary* describes 'motivation' as something which 'incites to action or determines the will'. This is an excellent, if somewhat simple, explanation. Management's role, if it truly desires a 'hot' sales force, is to approach the subject with careful preparation. Targets must not only be set. They must be explained. The overall company goal or philosophy must be expounded so that people know the 'why' as well as the 'what' of targeting.

This calls for an 'open' style of management and a constant dialogue between board, managers and salespeople, so that what is expected of them is clear and unequivocal. Salespeople hate being condescended to. 'Put another million on sales, young Fortesque, and I'll give you a voucher for a free weekend in Luton' is what I call the 'gold-watch-after-twenty-years--plus-a-chance-to-dance-with-the-chairman's-wife' kind of approach, and is utterly useless. Enlightened self-interest is the spur. Real rewards are the key, not placebos.

If salespeople are responsible enough to represent your company to the outside world, then they sure as hell are entitled to know about such things as cash flow, dividend policy, capital expenditure programmes, research and development and most other things.

Targets should never be too easy. But sometimes they do become easier to reach as the year progresses. At the start line, however, they should be stiff. They must require exceptional effort to reach – and they must be linked to tangible rewards.

If Joe Bognostravitch's fancy kettle company needs to sell 8 million kettles to break even, 8.5 million to make a small profit, and 9 million to make a good profit, pay dividends and poke a little into reserve, then the sales target should be, shall we say, 9.2 million for starters? If, through exceptional sweat and hard selling, those wonderful kettle salesmen turn in 10 million, then their improved earnings on bonus and commission should be significant. If they go berserk and hit 11 million (provided the cost of producing the extra product isn't too high) then they should be rewarded even more handsomely.

The sale of arms is not a fashionable subject. Guns can kill, and although every nation on earth buys guns, the seller of weapons is a bit of an outsider. Here is a cautionary tale, absolutely true incidentally, but I am compelled not to reveal names.

An arms salesman broke new markets in 1979 for his British company's products. He passed his sales target by a huge margin and as a consequence earned £78,000 and commission.

Result? Embarrassment. Shock. Horror. The fact that his company's profits soared was almost forgotten – the main problem was that the guy was too successful. He quit the next year and took up a job with an American outfit where he earns in the region of $150,000 to $200,000 a year. Over there he's a hero. Over here, he was OK, but, well really, you know – those kind of earnings are almost obscene.

The moral of the story? If you set targets and they are beaten by a mile, smile baby: your profits should have soared as well.

Here is a quotation lightly paraphrased from Adam Smith, the father of free enterprise who wrote his classic *The Wealth of Nations* over two hundred years ago.

It is not from the benevolence of the butcher, the baker or the brewer that we expect our dinner, but from their regard to their own self-interest.

When setting sales targets, it's useful to remember that desire is the beginning of all human achievement, and that soaring sales figures, springing from a disciplined company environment, are an umbilical cord attached to profitability. If one rises so should the other. If marketing men don't believe that, then where, pray, are we all heading for?

Furthermore, *Cassells English Dictionary* defines 'incentive' as being something which 'acts as a motive, incitement or spur'. If we take this description at its face value one could easily make out a case for thumbscrews or the lash as being excellent incentives.

However, I shall confine myself to those incentives that are at best supposed to galvanize the executives and work force of British industry to perform feats of Herculean super-productivity – or at worst to feather-bed the idle Anglo-Saxons on their downward slide to mediocrity.

First of all, let us be clear about one thing. A 'perk' is not the same as an incentive, although the dividing line is wafer thin. One man's incentive may well be no more than the expected norm for somebody else, and a degree of creative selectivity is needed if employers are to squeeze the last drop of benefit from their own, often neglected, side of the bargain.

Thus, when drawing up incentive schemes or bonus plans the employer should be crystal clear as to just what he or she hopes to obtain by introducing such wonders as free hairdressing, holidays in Morocco, crates of champagne or life membership of the Hounslow Ferret Sexing Association.

Now this is easy enough when assessing the 'reward-ethic' for salesmen. At its most simple, a company can decide what its expected profit will be and provide a scale of cash rewards for its sales force if they exceed these predetermined expectations. The trick is to set targets that are high enough to convince shareholders of their 'genuineness', and that the whole thing is not simply a sleazy rip-off dreamed up by the sales director to ingratiate himself with his 'team'.

In other words, incentive-linked targets should be tough. They shouldn't, on the other hand, be so ridiculously high they they are clearly out of reach. 'Impossible' targets are, in fact, a *dis*incentive and rapidly become counterproductive. My own personal philosophy is that *extra special rewards* should *only* be associated with *extra special results* and that provided the company's original targets are surpassed, it matters not a jot how much *more* the individual salesman earns.

Many people, as I have said, pay lip service to this as an ideal, but jib at its implementation. I am often accused of eccentrity when arguing this philosophy. 'What?' they cry. 'An individual salesman earning that much? Disgraceful! What about the differentials, the unions, the state of the British economy, the starving Chinese, my own non-incentive-linked salary, the effect on morale and elderly shareholders' blood pressure?'

Alternatively, an ill-conceived scheme which pays out at too low a level of performance will court anguish, disaster and sometimes a punch up the bracket at the next AGM.

'That's all very well!'. I hear the serried ranks of chartered accountants bellow. 'You can measure a salesman's perform-ance in hard cash, but what about the equally industrious clerical worker, computer operator or receptionist?' Not an easy question to answer. It is more difficult to measure performance in these kinds of jobs and then link them directly to rewards that are only paid when the performance norm is exceeded.

Difficult, but not impossible. I suspect that many departmental specialists have rarely set out logically what they believe to be high-quality performance whether it is speed of execution, neatness, lack of errors, or even simple punctuality.

A well-known advertising agency in New York has an elaborate 'points' system for all its staff, right down to the janitor. Excellence is measured in a variety of ways, but if the employee scores enough merit points in a month he or she can earn a substantial cash bonus. Staff strive to earn points and the company benefits from increased output, enthusiasm and general efficiency.

A word of caution. Incentives in my view should be over and above normal remuneration, not a crafty way of making staff run themselves ragged just to reach average earnings.

When introducing incentive schemes to staff, particular care should be taken to explain the downside risk as well as the magical potential. Salespeople are notoriously emotional about failure to reach targets, but if they do fail, whether through low performance or bad luck (strikes, illness, multiple pregnancies), they must be made to face the consequences.

I have often warned my own sales staff that bonus earnings can fall as well as rise, depending on market circumstances, and that prudence in managing their own financial affairs is essential. We are all familiar with the man or woman who 'assumes' next year's earnings in advance and straps on a giant mortgage, two holidays in Majorca, a Pierre Cardin suit and a small blonde with a flat in Putney. The small blonde, of course, can be male or female, according to preference, but whatever the gender you can be certain that Blondie will be expensive. Having issued warnings to sales staff about not living beyond their means, don't actually expect them to take any notice. Most salespeople overreach themselves financially, claiming, with some justification, that being in debt acts as a goad to greater effort. Think about it. Do you know many really good salespeople who live comfortably within their means and are content with a holiday in Macclesfield and a wonderfully styled, off-the-peg suit from Sainsbury's? You do? OK, buster, you hire them. I certainly won't.

Apart from cash incentives, what about other forms of reward? Company cars are usually perks, not incentives, but sales conferences in exotic locations are. Once again, the Americans lead the world in creative solutions to the problem of motivating staff to greater effort. A west coast publisher sends his top performers to Europe on an all-expenses-paid trip with their spouses. He also lets staff name specific items or products they covet, such as wall-to-wall yak-skin carpets, or a rubber frogman's suit for the mother-in-law, then constructs a points system which indicates how much effort they must put in to achieve their heart's desire. I was also told of a toy manufacturer who supplies friendly hostesses for his star male performers, and gigantic hairy football players for his star female performers. Presumably those staff who fail to reach target are paired off with gigantic hairy hostesses or weedy, knock-kneed football players with terminal halitosis.

Should rewards be based on team efforts or individual performance? There's no cut-and-dried answer to this question, as circumstances vary from company to company. In my own, it has to be team effort because accounts can change groups in mid-season, necessitating elaborate restructuring of targets. When I was selling baked beans for a famous but, in my view, chronically stingy company in the 1950s, I was always smashing sales targets in my East End territory and receiving letters that ran something like this:

Dear Turner

Congratulations! You've done it again! My goodness, you are a clever chap. Clearly we underestimated your ability when setting your current target and I know you will be flattered to hear that the company is therefore quadrupling it with immediate effect! Good luck and keep selling!

PS Your expenses are too high. Ten shillings for lunch is an extravagance you must learn to control.

In an ideal world the actual incentive would be different for every separate individual because, as I mentioned earlier, one man's bonus can be another man's norm. Newly married staff would probably choose cash, whereas the older, more established personnel might opt for goods or services, i.e., cheap car-purchase schemes, wardrobes full of clothes, relief massage, assisted showers.

Seriously though, if, as we are constantly told by the posh Sunday papers, Britain must increase productivity, or collapse giggling into the North Sea, then more companies must find solid reasons for all their staff to contribute to this increased productivity. In a free society, the best rewards should go to those who deliver and not, as so often happens, to those who have the most muscle. In the advertising business, which is no stranger to glittering prizes, incentives can often be corrupted into no more than a person's 'rights'

– with no corresponding guarantee of 'above norm' excellence from the employee.

We've all heard of the apocryphal interview at a glossy ad agency where the seventeen-year-old time-buyer was asking his prospective employer about fringe benefits. 'Well,' said the managing director, drawing languidly on his Balkan Sobranie, 'there's the ice-blue Porsche, with built-in sauna and blindfolded gipsy violinist, the thrice-yearly tax-free cash bonus, the nine-week seminar at the IPA summer school in Acapulco, the company penthouse for your exclusive use, the subsidized piano lessons, the eighty-thousand-pound mortgage at 2 per cent over forty years, the handcrafted jock-straps personalized with your own initials, the free access to our executive clinic in Gstaad which, as you know, specializes in cures for acne and the . . .' At this juncture, the time-buyer raised a Neanderthal paw. 'OK so far,' he drawled, experiencing difficulty with such a complicated sentence, 'but what 'appens if I'm actually successful at me job?'

Thus, incentives should be real, they should be truly desirable, they should be linked to high-octane performance and they should, if provided at all, be of benefit to the employer as well as to the employed. A thousand pounds' worth of extra bonus distributed among high-performers in a company is good news only if the company's targets have been genuinely surpassed and profits are ahead of expectations.

Finally, an example of the incentive syndrome taken to manic extremes. An investment sales manager of my acquaintance provides exotic holidays as a bonus for his most brilliantly successful sales staff, but requires all the other non-successful wretches who fell short of target to turn up at the airport and wave the star performers bon voyage. He usually arranges the flight departure to be on a Sunday morning at seven a.m. Ouch!

21. Promotion

Should you seek it?
And is there life after sales?

To be a good salesman means maintaining that engine inside you that drives upwards and onwards towards even greater goals. Naturally, as you become more successful, or, as the Americans say, 'achievement-orientated', you expect to be rewarded for that success.

One of the fatal mistakes a lot of companies make is to reward a top salesman by promoting him out of sales altogether. This is a dangerous strategy, and doubly so because it can damage both employee *and* company – sometimes permanently. The art of salesmanship is highly specialized and requires many interlocking skills, but there is no guarantee that a star salesman will automatically make a good manager. Or a brilliant sales director, or a competent managing director.

I know more than a handful of top salesmen who now sit behind chief executives' desks surrounded by secretaries and aides and personal assistants and other barriers against the outside world. Not all of them are happy. They miss the cut and thrust of selling and the company of other salespeople. They have been moved away from the coalface and cannot anymore utilize their skills to the maximum.

This is why smart chief executives keep their salesmen actually selling. They find other ways to reward their success – in addition to more money. They give them prestige titles like Vice-President-in-Charge-of-Sales. But they keep them at the coalface. It seems logical to me – but not everybody would agree.

Some years ago I was offered the chance to be joint managing director of my company. It would have meant moving out of sales completely and concentrating on such fascinating topics as labour relations, administration, corporate affairs (boring dinners with Lord Mayors and Lady Mayoresses) and the economics of subsidized canteen lunches. I politely declined, opting to stay with what I do best, and I've never regretted it for a moment.

There are, of course, many talented salesmen who have crossed the line and become brilliant chief executives, but the message should be clearly understood – *there is no guarantee against failure*. There is one thing worse than a top salesman floundering impotently in the uncomfortable straitjacket of a chief executive. And that is a narrow-minded, parsimonious, nit-picking accountant who has made it to the top. Mark you, if you find a *creative* accountant you've got a winner!

Engineers are almost as bad, but not quite. A lot depends, of course, on the individual company and the markets in which it operates. High technology firms need chief executives who are not technically illiterate, and TV or film companies need men and women who understand – and have a 'feel' for – show business. Hollywood's decline in the 1960s was due partly to relentless competition from television, but also because major studios panicked and put accountants in charge. Accountancy is a valuable discipline for *any* business, but its practitioners are *trained not to have imagination*. They are by nature conservative, and abhor risk-taking. Indeed, too many chief executives in modern business won't go to the lavatory unless their research department or computer printout tells them it's OK.

You may, however, be a salesman who regards selling as a stepping stone to general management and be prepared to absorb the wider, more esoteric disciplines of marketing and ultimate profit responsibility. If you are, good luck to you. There is room at the top for such people, but if you are only interested in a selling career then try and avoid being seduced by fancy titles into a job you may live to bitterly regret.

The best parallel I can think of to drive this point home conclusively is the actor who wants to direct. I always shudder when I hear a fine professional actor chuntering away on television about his desire to abandon what he does best and 'direct'.

So, if you're running a company and you have a bunch of hot-shot salesmen who are performing superbly, it is *your responsibility to keep them at it*. They must be constantly remotivated, encouraged, rewarded and recognized.

But don't move them from the coalface. Salesmen have *two* particularly dominant personality traits: ego-drive and empathy. Ego-drive is the urge to succeed – sometimes it transcends all other considerations. If it is not balanced by empathy it can be a destructive force. Empathy is about sensitivity to the reactions and feelings of others. It is the creative spark that makes the truly great salesman. Chief executives and sales directors should nurture the two qualities like hothouse plants. A number of academic studies have attempted to quantify empathy and ego-drive, without much success. Most people have a degree of both in them, but where they are *marked* in an individual, the chances are he or she will make a good salesman or saleswoman.

Very few people have both these qualities in equal proportions and this is where the problems arise. Strong empathy and reduced drive means less 'cutting edge' which will make the closing of sales difficult. Too much ego-drive and too little empathy produces the killer instinct and very little else. The overriding lust for success will cause such a person to bully and cajole rather than persuade and, in the long run, real business achievement will elude them. (For those people with both *low* ego-drive and *low* empathy, selling, as a career, would be hell on earth.)

In summary, therefore, provided you are continuously excited by your work and your company recognizes and rewards you handsomely, there is no reason why you shouldn't remain in pure selling for the whole of your business life. Even if you end up being called Senior-

Vice-President-and-Executive-Director-Responsible-for-Customer-and-Company-Interface. You think that's a title I've just invented, don't you? Well, it isn't. I know an American salesman in the real estate jungle of southern California who luxuriates in *just* such a title. He needs very wide visiting cards? He also makes a cool half a million dollars a year. Think about *that* the next time you are tempted to hang up your briefcase and move to the womb-like security of head office as a general manager!

22. Marketing and Selling
Are they the same thing?

It has become fashionable these days for manufacturers of rivets, chocolate, soup, razor blades and foaming pessaries to describe themselves not as purveyors of the aforementioned products, but simply as 'marketing' companies. What do they mean? The definition adopted by the Institute of Marketing is as follows:

> The management function which organizes and directs all those business activities involved in assessing and converting customer purchasing power into effective demand for a specific product or service to the final consumer or user so as to achieve the profit, target or other objectives set by a company (that is, the presentation and distribution of goods and services in the manner best designed to benefit the producer, the distributor and the public).

Have you got that?

In many companies, the function of marketing and that of selling are still inextricably entwined. The pure marketing manager is attempting to initiate and control his company's marketing activity whilst also trying to direct the sales team out on the territory. This often leads to confusion and a diminution of effort.

Years ago, men of vision like Thomas Edison and King Gillette created products which they virtually 'willed' into existence. The extent of their marketing expertise was to decide – almost single-handedly – to produce an item that the mass market would respond to. These men followed 'hunches', took breathtaking chances and finally conquered the world with their determination to succeed.

But the world has changed. Entrepreneurs do still exist – men like Freddie Laker, who will succeed again, and Alan Bond, the Australian tycoon who took Australia to victory in the America's Cup. They have charisma – and a ruthless, buccaneering style. Their business talents are as much instinctive as academic. They are old-fashioned *salesmen*.

Modern marketing man is a different animal. Charisma? He thinks charisma is an Indian restaurant in Surbiton. Buccaneering? That's in old black-and-white movies on TV. Modern marketing man is often dull, studious, safe, careful. He does everything by the book. But, although his type doesn't get *my* adrenaline flowing, I won't condemn him out of hand.

Big business is now exceedingly complex; there is a compelling need for high-volume sales, and the degree of competition between manufacturers is so keen that only the most economical methods of design and production will maintain profitability. This high-volume, low-cost requirement leads to another vital ingredient in the mix – a constant supply of consumers conditioned to make repeat purchases in the market place.

The marketing manager, continuously pressed on the one had to contain *costs*, is also being squeezed to rack up *higher* profits for his company each year. He is obsessed, therefore, with effecting economies of scale, i.e., with finding more and more consumers to justify increased production. He now oversees product development, research, packaging, warehousing, distribution, trade margins, advertising. All these disparate functions are interconnected – indeed, they are all vital one to the other, like links in a great chain.

So, modern marketing man, with his off-the-peg suit and his Volvo Estate and his four-bedroom mock Georgian house and his huge mortgage and his golf club fees he can't afford, is a billion light years away from being a pure salesman. His job – poor, balding, lager-drinking, Majorca-holidaying bastard – is becoming more comprehensive by the *day*. It is now concerned with everything from inception, design, pricing, distribution, promotion and merchandising until his product, whether it be a can of soup or a block of salt, drops with a satisfying plop into Mrs Housewife's shopping basket.

It is therefore blindingly obvious that *marketing* – as it is now understood – embraces a whole lot more than simply selling the product. It must identify *what* product should be made, *how* it should be sold, *when* it should be sold, *where* it should be sold, *how much* it should be sold for, and of course *to whom* it should be sold.

The logistics of distribution are now so complicated that manufacturers need to look beyond the good will of wholesalers for their market intelligence, and most business plans these days are based upon scientifically collated statistics rather than managerial 'hunch'.

Research is a business tool that modern marketing man regards as an omnipotent Holy Grail. He is unlikely to risk *his real personal judgement* if it flies in the face of the research findings. This is understandable. Up to a point. Modern marketing man is rarely an entrepreneur. He is a salaried employee who has been trained in much the same way as his chief accountant. *Thoroughly*. And often, alas, unimaginatively.

He must address himself, usually through his research department, to the behaviour of his competitors. He must judge their current performance against his own, anticipate their next moves, assess what, if any, counterclaim he must recommend. He must keep a crucial lifeline to the actual *consumers* of his product. Are their needs being met? And at the right price? Do they have brand loyalty? Can advertising *create* new *wants*? Or switch loyalties? Are the big retailing chains like Tesco and Sainsbury competing with his established brand names by offering similar own-label goods in their stores? Should his company offer to make such own-label products as well? And if they do, how will it squeeze his already hard-pressed margins?

He will have to do all this, and *more*. There are merchandising, promotions, demonstrations, price offers, free trials, trade mark-ups, and gap analyses to be worried about too. Little wonder, then, that when it comes to recruiting, training and motivating a sales force, the marketing man is too knackered or confused to pay much attention to such a peripheral 'end activity'!

The role of a powerful *sales director*, therefore, becomes paramount. His role in the highly sophisticated manufacturing company is to bring very special human skills to the job. He alone can demonstrate the importance of *pure salesmanship* in the total marketing mix. He will insist that his salesmen use their personalities and their power of persuasion to create 'good will' among customers.

He will try to 'humanize' the dry-as-dust research reports and identify the USPs (Unique Selling Propositions) that lurk like golden nuggets amongst the computer printouts. The sales director can only do this effectively if he is not also expected to be grappling with all those other myriad duties I have outlined. It is only a good sales director who will understand the psychological importance of *timing* in a sales situation.

Some years ago, an advertising man, Michael Keefe, now Managing Director of Gerrards, invented a phrase – 'the Emotional Buying Trigger' or EBT. This was some item or phrase in the sales proposition that literally 'triggered' off the buying response. Salesmen are always hunting for this trigger – and squeezing it gently when they do find it.

Where the pure *salesman* differs from the pure *marketing* man is often on an emotional level, although more and more exercises these days straddle both disciplines. Marketing, as a concept, now necessarily invades a lot of other territory inside a company. This can, and does, cause a lot of angst, jealousy, suspicion and, occasionally, hysteria.

But if a marketing man is to function at all, he has to

involve himself in research, production, finance, sales and all the rest of the company's hitherto sacrosanct priest-holes. I have no doubt that a sound marketing strategy is essential for survival in the eighties – provided that strategy includes the encouragement of enthusiastic, determined and well-informed *salesmanship* in its purest, most dynamic form.

A marketing plan, however well researched and documented, will not shift merchandise by itself. Products will not leap off the shelves of the supermarket simply because the marketing director has got all his sums right. Somewhere down the line an act of selling has to take place.

And don't you believe all that nonsense about computers taking over the sales function by the end of this century. That is drivelling claptrap put about by ambitious computer *salesmen* with their eye on the main chance. Salesmen and saleswomen will be needed in the future more than ever before.

During a recent visit to Las Vegas, Nevada, I saw a magnificently crude sign tacked up outside an old hardware store. It was written in the proprietor's broad hand and was, in fact, a recruitment ad for sales staff. It read:

I want –
A whole heap of foot-tapping, finger-snapping, knee-cracking, ball-crunching, shit-kicking, no-nonsense salesman.
If *you* apply, you better be *real* good!

I find that curiously refreshing.

An old friend of mine, Peter Marsh, Chairman of one of Britain's biggest advertising agencies – Allen, Brady & Marsh – is himself a great salesman and showman, and although research plays a major role in his company's strategy, he reminds everybody that the most valuable quality a businessman can possess is 'persistence'.

Peter is particularly fond of quoting the famous Calvin Coolidge statement:

Nothing in this world can take the place of persistence. Talent will not; nothing is more common than unsuccessful men with talent. Genius will not. Unrewarded genius is almost a proverb. Education will not – the world is full of educated derelicts. Persistence and determination alone are omnipotent. The slogan 'press on' has solved and will always solve the problems of the human race.

That may or may not be an overstatement, depending upon your point of view, but it's sure as hell an *optimistic* slogan.

So be optimistic. The world of business is now more complicated than it was in the days when Adam Smith wrote his *Wealth of Nations* or Dale Carnegie his *How to Win Friends and Influence People*, but the role of salesmanship remains the same. Selling is the real dynamic force of marketing because it is the only part of the mix that actually *produces* revenue. Other activities have their role, of course, but none of them makes the cash register ring with the same degree of urgency. In the long history of trading the act of selling has always been the apex or the pinnacle of effort. It still is.

Today, more than ever, the salesman must zero in on the deep-seated desires of his customers. He must be alert to the fact that people purchase 'benefits', real or imagined, when they make a purchasing decision. He must continuously utilize all his 'personality' and 'human' skills in his day-to-day work. He must *not* be contemptuous of modern marketing man or his methods. They exist to help him be even more effective in his sales activity.

Think of how much *more* successful those early sales pioneers would have been if they had been supported by a sophisticated marketing machine. Men like Henry Ford, F. W. Woolworth and H. J. Heinz, who made personal fortunes anyway, would have been so rich you wouldn't have been able to count their money in a month of Sundays.

So, while marketing is a management process which

identifies, anticipates and meets consumer needs efficiently and profitably, always remember that *no product ever really sells itself*. It's you and me, sunshine, who do that.

So stay sharp, and keep selling.

Last Words

Selling the intangible and the ephemeral

Why inquisitiveness is good for you and other home truths

The fundamental qualities that go into creating a really great salesman are much the same whether he is selling motorcars, life insurance, processed food, oil or package holidays. As I suggested in an earlier chapter, the choice of *what* you sell is one of the most important decisions you will ever make. Get *that* right and most other problems will diminish with time and experience. Pick the *wrong* thing to sell – wrong for *you* that is – and you might just as well take up nude hang-gliding in Antarctica, for all the good it will do you.

The largest part of my own career has been in selling the ephemeral: space in newspapers and magazines, for example, and for the past twenty-one years – perhaps the most perishable and transient commodity in the world – time.

Stated simply and without embellishment it does sound a rather curious thing on which to have built a richly rewarding career. But I have been involved in selling television time – the commercial minutes that punctuate your ITV programmes and which in recent years have been filled with some of the most compelling and brilliant vignettes that our top creative minds could devise.

Airtime is a commodity market like no other on earth. Because no more than an average of six minutes of commercials can appear in each programming hour, airtime is a scarce resource. And it is highly perishable. It cannot be stored or kept on a shelf until tomorrow, unlike many other products. Its value – dependent on the size or quality, or both, of the TV audience watching *at any one time* –

is as a consequence, highly volatile.

But the actual minutes allocated for commercial breaks are no more than a vehicle for a series of sophisticated and dramatically variable messages aimed at the millions of people who watch television in the relaxed privacy of their own homes. The challenge and excitement of selling commercial airtime springs from the enormous variety of clients, products and services that the airtime salesman comes into contact with.

It is not uncommon to open a working day with a meeting that involves, shall we say, a processed food manufacturer. By mid-morning the salesman's attention will have switched to a life insurance company, lunch may well be with the agent of a foreign car importer, or a publisher of *Teach Yourself Carpentry* partworks. The afternoon could involve discussions with men who wish to sell ice cream, computers, sheepskin coats, razor blades or detergents. The variety is enormous.

Of course, to say we just sell 'minutes' of airtime is an over-simplification. What we are selling is 'people's attention' – a ferociously difficult commodity to trap, hold or quantify. We are selling audiences in large or small numbers. We are selling 'types' of audiences, whether young or old or rich or not-so-rich, and we are selling them in a highly complex range of mixes and combinations.

And our customers are engaged in the act of selling, too. They are competing for the attention of a large, critical, sophisticated population who are exposed to literally hundreds of selling propositions every day of their lives. They have to fight hard to get a 'share of shout' in the market place – and not all of them succeed.

There's an old tale advertising men used to tell about the poor farmer who saved hard all his life to buy what he had always desired – a really top-class mule. Eventually, after years of penny-pinching, he went to market and paid three thousand pounds for a prime beast. Sleek of coat and firm of haunch. Strong. And stubborn.

When he got it back to his ramshackle farm it wouldn't move. Try as he might, the wretched creature refused to budge. Exasperated, he sought the services of a local mule trainer. The trainer arrived and insisted on pre-payment of fifty pounds which the poor farmer had to borrow from his wife, having cleaned out his savings on the mule.

'OK,' he said glumly, 'go ahead and train the beggar.'

The mule trainer picked up a forty-five-pound sledge-hammer and hit the mule a tremendous blow between the eyes. The animal keeled over stone dead with his skull split open like a pomegranate. The poor farmer went crazy. 'What the hell have you done?' he yelled. 'I paid you to train the mule, *not* to knock his brains out!'

The mule trainer gave a resigned shrug. 'I was only trying to get his attention *first*,' he explained.

So, take it easy. Don't knock the brains out of your customers. You need to get their attention, of course. But if you come on *too* strong you'll never win their confidence. You're more likely to earn a punch in the throat.

Furthermore, if selling is the career *you* choose, try and identify the product or service that you believe will keep your adrenaline accelerating. If enthusiasm is to be infectious, it *has* to be genuine.

Knowledge is strength, and for a salesman there is no better way to acquire it, and to go on acquiring it, than by reading. Read as many newspapers as you can. Treat yourself to at least *two* of the international weeklies like the *Economist* and *Newsweek*. Buy books whenever you can afford them – and occasionally when you can't. Devour novels, autobiographies, thrillers, comedies, ghost stories and political essays. Over the years your store of knowledge will slowly increase – *without you needing to undertake any formal study*.

As your selling career progresses, you will make contact with people at an ever-increasing level of seniority in business. You must develop social skills as well as persuasive skills. You must learn to listen, to absorb and to digest. Don't be afraid to be a sponge and borrow from people their best ideas, the cream of their knowledge and the distillation of their experience.

There are, remember, very few *entirely original* concepts in business today. They may at first glance *seem* highly original, but in truth they are like the visible apex of an iceberg – built on layers you *cannot* see. The American spacecraft, in all their technical magnificence, are no more than great-great-great-grandchildren of the wheel.

So, be inquisitive. It's a marvellous quality to have. All great men and women have possessed it in abundance. Churchill, Marie Curie, Ralph Waldo Emerson, Dale Carnegie – they all remained *curious* until they died. And so must the man or woman who takes up selling as a career. Being inquisitive will help you develop another positive quality: an interest in other people's lives. Not just the rich and powerful, but the young and struggling, the janitor as well as the tycoon. People *are* interesting – and human and fallible just like you.

Impose some form of order in your life where you can. Be punctual in business, answer your mail, eat and sleep regularly, and use your energy for accomplishing your life's goals.

And don't be afraid to list your life's goals either. Write down a personalized ten-year plan of where you want to be at the end of that period. Achievement starts when you say to yourself, 'I can do it.' You don't have a *chance* of success if you allow life to toss you around like a cork in a storm.

Try to think less about your problems, and what you can't do, and concentrate on what you are *about to achieve*. If you can manage not to dwell on problems for a single day, you will make fascinating discoveries about yourself. I know it is said that a problem shared is a problem halved, but why not share a bit of optimism and joy with your long-suffering friends for a change? Try, if you can, to spend more time with people who are energetic and hopeful. Energy and hope are highly contagious So are misery and defeatism. And you *can* choose.

Avoid the trap of only making friends among your own age group. Some of your most joyous relationships can be with the very young and the very old.

Savour and enjoy all those transient moments of intensity in life as if they were lifebelts tossed to a drowning man. If you have long nursed a desire to ride bareback past the great Egyptian pyramids in Cairo – what's stopping you? I did it. And I was relatively poor at the time.

Develop an interest in travel. Most top salesmen have a restless quality anyway, and in these days of package holidays you can – in stages – see more of the world in *your* lifetime than Marco Polo did during his!

Don't let fear of ultimate failure daunt you – particularly at the outset of your career. Quite often fear of failure is actually a *fear of success you may not be able to handle*. Does that sound crazy to you?

Think about it for a moment. All of us at some time have worried we might have 'bitten off more than we could chew'. We are occasionally paranoid about scaling a height from which we can tumble ignominiously. If you plan to tackle one goal at a time you will soon overcome this fear. Each small step forward will reinforce your confidence and before very long you will be leaping tall buildings without hesitation. Remember that quitting only weakens your resolve – and makes it harder to face the next task. *Going on* gives you a commitment to success.

And always remember that success is a *personal* thing. It is *your* assessment of success that counts – not other people's. However you drive yourself, you will always see others in the fast lane going like the clappers. *It doesn't matter*.

What matters is how you are handling *your* goals. Don't be blown off course by somebody who bears no relationship to *your* life. Each of us has a particular view of success, and, although there are likely to be some similarities, one man's glittering achievement may well be treated with disdain by another. So set your *own* life targets.

And don't forget to *reward yourself* for each new target conquered. Even a half-bottle of champagne consumed in the bath will make an *occasion* of your success and if you get into the *habit* of creating a cycle of achievement-reward-achievement you will find your performance improving and your hunger for success becoming even sharper.

The title of this book is *The Gentle Art of Salesmanship*. Why *Gentle*? How does 'gentle' stack up with all these other 'sock-it-to-them' qualities we've discussed in previous chapters?

Simple, really. At the end of the day the truly great salesman will have persuaded the buyer to 'buy'. His act of salesmanship will be virtually undetectable. It will be the customer who makes the decision and it will be the skill of the salesman who makes him believe that it was his decision and his alone, that brought the transaction to a satisfactory conclusion.

This is the true pinnacle of the salesman's art and it takes patience, sweat and persistence to reach that state of the art. Some can do it by radiating enthusiasm, others by a skilful use of words, others by a demonstration, or by displaying extraordinary knowledge of what they sell, but all of them – throughout the length and breadth of the world – will know that people only *buy* if they believe in the *benefits* of what the salesman is promising.

They will buy if what is sold offers value for money, social status, health, power, relief from suffering, advantage over rivals, sexual charisma, career enhancement, joy, nutrition and respect. The gentle art of salesmanship is about investing *your* product or service with as many of those qualities as possible. It's about selling the 'sizzle' not the sausage. It's about creating wants and rekindling smouldering desires, it's about promising *and* delivering benefits, tangible *or* intangible, to your customers, as often as you can.

But no school of salesmanship, no book or course of study, no qualification etched on old parchment and sealed with wax will ever be a substitute for real experience because, when all is said and done, salesmanship is about *performance*, and the will to win.

Let's finish with a quotation from Conrad Hilton, the famous hotelier, which sums up the role of selling in the modern world.

Never give up, and never under any circumstances deceive anybody. Have your word good.

Index

Index